DATE DUE			

LANDMARK SUPREME COURT CASES

DON LAWSON

ENSLOW PUBLISHERS, INC.

Bloy St. & Ramsey Ave.   P.O. Box 38
Box 777   Aldershot
Hillside, N.J. 07205   Hants GU12 6BP
U.S.A.   U.K.

Library of Congress Cataloging in Publication Data

Lawson, Don.
    Landmark Supreme Court cases.

    Bibliography: p.
    Includes index.
    Summary: Discusses nine landmark Supreme Court cases, addressing such issues as desegregation of schools and the Miranda case, and considers the future of the Supreme Court.
    1. United States –Constitutional law –Cases –Juvenile literature. 2. Civil rights–United States –Cases– Juvenile literature. 3. United States. Supreme Court. [1. United States–Constitutional law. 2. Civil rights. 3. United States. Supreme Court] I. Title.
KF4550.Z9L393 1987 342.73'085'02648 86-19735
ISBN 0-89490-132-X   347.3028502648

Printed in the United States of America

10 9 8 7 6 5 4 3 2

Illustration Credits
The Bettmann Archive, p. 25; Courtesy Supreme Court Historical Society, pp. 6, 15, 27, 45, 98; Wide World Photos, pp. 36, 51, 71, 77, 105, 113, 120.

Acknowledgment

The author thanks Professor William M. Beaney of the College of Law at the University of Denver for his review of the manuscript and for his helpful suggestions.

Contents

The United States Supreme Court Building in Washington, D.C.

1

It "Ain't Nothin' Until I Call It"

One of the great Chief Justices of the United States Supreme Court, Charles Evans Hughes, was a great baseball fan. He liked to tell the story about his favorite baseball umpire who settled disputed plays by declaring, "A play ain't *nothin'* until I call it. And what I call it, it is!"

Then Hughes would go on to explain that the Supreme Court was like that umpire: "We are under a Constitution, but the Constitution is what the Supreme Court justices say it is."

This was not always true. In fact, in the early days of its existence the Supreme Court played a relatively minor role in the nation's government. It simply interpreted what the Founding Fathers probably meant when they wrote the Constitution in 1787.

In the beginning there were not many such interpretations to be made. But as the United States grew and changed, the challenges to the Constitution steadily increased. By responding strongly to those challenges the Supreme Court helped keep the Constitution up to date. And gradually the Supreme Court became the most powerful court in the world.

The Supreme Court is provided for in the United States Constitution. Article III begins: "The judicial power of the United States shall be vested in one Supreme Court . . ." That simple statement indicates the genius of the Founding Fathers. Nowhere did they lay down a prescription for such details as what the Supreme Court was supposed to do, how many members there were to be, or when and where it was supposed to meet.

The Founding Fathers were wise enough to know that because future generations would be called upon to deal with changing times and changing situations, the Constitution had to be flexible. The Supreme Court has perhaps met this test of flexibility better than any other instrument of government. Successive Courts have not hesitated to correct what they have regarded as errors or oversights of previous Courts.

The number of Supreme Court justices varied between six and ten until after the Civil War. Then today's total of nine was permanently established. During the New Deal era in the 1930s President Franklin D. Roosevelt attempted to increase their number. By doing so Roosevelt hoped to appoint enough new justices who were sympathetic with his New Deal legislation to gain favorable Supreme Court decisions on whether or not this legislation was constitutional. But congressional opponents of this "court-packing" scheme, supported by several individual justices, killed the measure in Congress.

All of the Supreme Court members—a Chief Justice and eight associate justices—are appointed by the president and must be confirmed by the Senate. They may remain in office for life, subject only to good behavior. Any questions of a justice's conduct must be determined by the Senate. In 1987, there had been 105 Supreme Court justices, beginning with John Jay, through Sandra Day O'Connor—the first woman ever appointed to the Court—to Antonin Scalia.

The matter of lifetime tenure has its positive and negative sides. On the positive side is the fact that, once appointed, a justice does not have to worry about how his decisions may affect his remaining in office. This sense of job security has occasionally brought surprising results. From time to time a justice appointed because of his liberal or conservative philosophy has confounded the president who appointed him by suddenly rendering decisions against that administration's legislation and directly opposed to his own earlier liberal or conservative reputation. Such renegade action is relatively rare, but it is a healthy indication that the Supreme Court is truly an independent body.

The negative side of lifetime tenure has mainly to do with a justice's continued physical and mental ability to perform his Supreme Court duties. The job calls for a topflight legal mind and, especially in recent years, physical endurance that will help a justice stand up under an ever-increasing case load. Any physical or mental impairments such as those which all too frequently accompany advancing age may well lead to a justice's being a hindrance to the Court. Few justices, no matter how seriously incapacitated, have voluntarily stepped down from the Supreme Court. The job of justice is one of great prestige and power, and it also pays very well—about $100,000 a year. As a result, death rather than retirement usually removes a Supreme Court justice from his job.

Almost without exception Supreme Court justices have been dedicated to upholding the Court's motto, "Equal Justice Under Law." Those words are carved over the entrance to the temple-like building that has been the Court's home since 1935. Before that it was housed in a few small rooms in the basement of the nation's Capitol. Space there was so cramped that before the justices sat down to go to work they had to put on their robes in public. From the Capitol basement the Court moved to the former U.S. Senate chambers and from there to its present handsome quarters. Fronted by rows of tall Corinthian columns, the marble building is located at one edge of a plaza east of the Capitol.

As an indication of the historic honesty and integrity of Supreme Court justices, there have seldom been demands that any of them be removed from office. In the 1950s and 1960s Chief Justice Earl Warren was widely criticized by political conservatives for his consistently liberal opinions and decisions. This criticism soon extended to the other justices, whom the conservative public accused of being unduly influenced by Warren. Gradually an "Impeach the Warren Court" movement was formed, and impeachment bumper stickers and signboards began to appear across the land. The Senate, however, ignored these demands, and soon the movement died out.

Only one justice has ever been impeached. In 1804 Samuel Chase, a political opponent of President Thomas Jefferson, was accused of making libelous and seditious statements about the Jefferson administration. Chase, one of the signers of the Declaration of Independence, was tried by the Senate but quickly acquitted, and his acquittal helped to establish the independence of the Supreme Court. Had Chase been found guilty, later chief executives and their administrations undoubtedly would have attempted to remove any and all Supreme Court justices who handed down opinions against proposed legislation. President Franklin Roosevelt's effort to outmaneuver the Court by adding justices rather than removing them from office proved equally unsuccessful and has not been tried since.

Chase was serving on the Supreme Court during the early years of the legendary John Marshall's lengthy term as Chief Justice. Marshall, the fourth Chief Justice, had been appointed to that position in 1801 by President John Adams. Until Marshall's day the Court had such a poor reputation that few men wanted to serve on it. In fact, John Jay, the first Chief Justice, who was appointed by President Washington, later resigned from the job, saying that the Court lacked "weight, energy, and dignity." However, Marshall, who is still referred to by lawyers and historians as "the Great Chief Justice," soon transformed the Court into a highly respected third branch of the government fully equal to the executive and legislative branches.

During John Marshall's thirty-four years as Chief Justice one of the most important cases brought before the Supreme Court was the one known as *Marbury versus Madison*. (The word *versus* comes from Latin and means "against." In court cases it is usually abbreviated as "v." or "vs.") *Marbury v. Madison*, which started out as a small, apparently unimportant dispute, is still referred to in Supreme Court cases today.

2

John Marshall and *Marbury* v. *Madison*

John Marshall, born in a log cabin in Virginia in 1755, was the eldest of fifteen children. Although he had little early formal education, his mother and father had both been well educated in England before coming to America, and they conducted a regular frontier classroom for their children.

John's father, Thomas Marshall, was a close friend of George Washington's and had helped Washington survey Virginia. Thomas was also an ardent patriot and strongly supported the colonial movement for independence from England. He instilled this patriotic spirit in his large family, especially his eldest son, John.

In 1755 there were armed clashes between the British troops and the colonists, and young John and his father fought as Minutemen in these clashes in Virginia. When the Revolutionary War actually began, John joined the Continental Army, serving under Washington for several years in New Jersey, New York, and Pennsylvania. The harsh winter at Valley Forge tested the Continental Army's loyalty and courage. Afterwards John said, "I went into the Revolution a Virginian and came out an American."

After the Revolution John studied law at the College of William and Mary, was licensed to practice in 1780, and shortly afterwards established a law practice in Richmond, Virginia. He was elected to the state house of delegates, a body similar to today's state legislature. For the next decade he gained increasing stature as a successful lawyer. He was also a strong supporter of the proposed national constitution and fought for its ratification. Since Virginia was then the largest and most populous state, it played a key role in that contest. One of the opponents of ratification was the great orator Patrick Henry, whose "Give me liberty or give me death" speech had done much to spark the Revolution. Marshall was a match for Henry in the prolonged debate over the constitution, and on June 25, 1788, Virginia voted by a narrow margin to ratify the document. A month later New York, led by Alexander Hamilton, also voted for ratification, and the United States Constitution became, at least in theory, the law of the land.

As a reward for Marshall's efforts, newly installed President Washington offered him the position of United States attorney for Virginia. Marshall turned the job down, however, preferring to serve in Virginia's house of delegates as a supporter of the national government and the state's leader of the Federalist party. He also later turned down several other proposed federal appointments, but in 1800 President John Adams offered him the post of Secretary of State and he accepted.

Marshall had served as Secretary of State for only a few months when the Chief Justice of the Supreme Court, Oliver Ellsworth, was forced to resign because of ill health. President Adams appointed Marshall in his place, and Marshall was confirmed as Chief Justice by the Senate on January 27, 1801. Temporarily, he also continued to serve as secretary of state.

John Marshall became the first Chief Justice on January 27, 1801. During his term, the Supreme Court issued more than 11,000 opinions, half of which were written by Marshall himself.

The Chief Justice's job was admirably suited both to Marshall's great abilities as a lawyer and to his philosophy of government. He passionately believed that under the Constitution the United States was not merely a loose federation of states but a nation bound together by federal laws. But even the federal laws, Marshall believed, were not valid if they conflicted with the Constitution. The first great case in which the Supreme Court headed by Marshall took a giant step toward establishing the reality of the Constitution as the supreme law of the land occurred in 1803. This was *Marbury* v. *Madison.*

Marbury v. Madison

John Adams had been defeated for reelection to the presidency by Thomas Jefferson in November 1800. Just before he left office Adams appointed forty-two justices of the peace for the District of Columbia. In those days these jobs were federal appointments.

All of the commissions naming the new appointees had been signed, and the United States seal had been stamped on them before Jefferson took office. But not all of the commissions had been delivered, and many historians believe that Jefferson held up the delivery of at least some of them so he could name his own appointees. One of the men who had been named a federal justice of the peace by Adams but who did not receive his actual commission was a man named William Marbury.

Marbury went to the office of the new Secretary of State, James Madison, a Jefferson appointee and also a future president, and demanded his commission. When Madison refused to give it to him, Marbury brought suit in the United States Supreme Court itself against Madison on the grounds that withholding the signed and sealed commission was illegal.

Behind this cat-and-mouse game with the signed but un-delivered commissions was the bitter political struggle going on between defeated ex-President Adams and newly elected President Jefferson. The conservative Adams was head of the Federalist party. The liberal—some even said radical—Jefferson headed the Democratic-Republican party. Adams and many of his fellow Federalists were firmly convinced that Jefferson and his radical followers would destroy the newly founded United States if they were not somehow kept under control. That was why Adams, shortly before leaving office, had appointed loyal Federalists to the forty-two justice of the peace jobs. Now it would be up to Chief Justice Marshall, himself a staunch Federalist, and the rest of the Supreme Court, to decide if the Adams appointments were legally binding on Adams's successor, President Jefferson.

Actually, of course, what Adams had done was pack the federal judiciary in Washington, D.C., just as New Deal President Franklin Roosevelt would later attempt to pack the Supreme Court. But that was not the issue around which the *Marbury* v. *Madison* case was decided. To begin with, Chief Justice Marhsall was at a distinct disadvantage in proving to the American public that the case was being tried in an unprejudiced manner. Many modern observers have said that Marshall should have disqualified himself from even taking part in the case, since he had been the secretary of state as well as Chief Justice when the commissions in question had been signed by the secretary of state's office. And since Marshall was also widely known as a Federalist leader everyone expected him to come down firmly in favor of the Marbury claim.

Equally important, the Supreme Court at this time had none of the authority and prestige it commands today. Few cases of any importance had come before the Court or had been decided by it. Consequently, it had little precedent on which to base its decisions and no assurance that those decisions would be acted upon. (A later president, Andrew Jackson, was to challenge the Court by saying, "The Supreme Court has made its decision—now let the Chief Justice try and enforce it." Because of precedents established by Marshall, however, Jackson was unable to make his challenge stick.)

Chief Justice Marshall was well aware that public opinion would be all important in the Supreme Court's ruling in the *Marbury* v. *Madison* case. To begin with, if the Supreme Court merely issued a legal order—called a *writ of mandamus*—declaring that Marbury had a right to his justice of the peace commission, President Jefferson probably would simply ignore the order. And since Jefferson was such an enormously popular president, the public in general and Congress in particular would undoubtedly support Jefferson. What was more, Marshall realized, such an act on his part might well result in his own impeachment.

Technically, Marshall had a right at that time to issue such a *writ of mandamus*. The authority had been given to the Supreme Court by the Congressional Judiciary Act of 1789. But now it was on this very act that Marshall based his historic decision by performing what since has been regarded as the neatest judicial trick of the nineteenth century. He did so by declaring the Judiciary Act unconstitutional. "In other words," as historian John A. Garraty has pointed out, "Congress did not have the legal right to give that power to the Court!"

Marshall went on to claim that the Supreme Court, according to the Constitution, did not even have the authority to hear such cases as *Marbury* v. *Madison*. The Supreme Court's main function, Marshall said, was to hear cases that were brought before it on appeal after they had been tried in a lower court.

In his decision Marshall went on to state that Marbury had every right to his justice of the peace commission and that in withholding it Secretary of State Madison was "acting in plain violation of the law of the land." But, since the Judiciary Act was unconstitutional and thus the Supreme Court had no power to issue a *writ of mandamus,* it was not possible for the Supreme Court to force Madison—or Jefferson—finally to issue Marbury his commission.

In a very real sense Marshall came down on both sides of the fence in the *Marbury* v. *Madison* case. Marbury did not get his commission—he went on to become a successful local banker—but the more important thing was that for the very first time the U.S. Supreme Court had declared an act of Congress unconstitutional. And even President Jefferson did not dispute the Court's right to do so.

Almost immediately this gave the Supreme Court increased stature, and it was on the way toward becoming the supreme arbiter of American laws that it is today.

The Founding Fathers were insistent that there be three equally powerful divisions of American government—the executive, the legislative, and the judicial. Before John Marshall the judicial branch had remained in the shadows; after him it too emerged into the powerful light of equality.

During his term as Chief Justice the Supreme Court issued more than 11,000 opinions, half of which were written by Marshall himself. Almost singlehandedly not only did he establish the power of the Supreme Court to declare federal, state, and chief executive acts unconstitutional through the process of judicial review, but he also made it clear that federal power must prevail over state power if the two were ever in conflict. As historian Leonard Baker, Marshall's biographer, has pointed out, "Under Marshall the Supreme Court sought and achieved a moral force as great as that obtained by the presidency and the Congress."

But following the *Marbury* v. *Madison* decision it would be more than half a century before another act of Congress was declared unconstitutional by the Supreme Court. That was a decision in the *Dred Scott* v. *Sandford* case of March 1857, a decision that did much to start the American Civil War and of which later Supreme Court justices were far from proud. In fact, New Deal Supreme Court Justice Felix Frankfurter once said that he and his colleagues "never mentioned the Dred Scott case any more than a family in which a son had been hanged mentioned ropes and scaffolds."

3

The Dred Scott Case

Supreme Court justices pride themselves on basing their decisions on points of law rather than the personalities or circumstances of the people involved in cases brought before the nation's top tribunal. Thus the people behind many Supreme Court decisions are greatly overshadowed by the historical results of their decisions. As one former Justice, Potter Stewart, has said, "Supreme Court Justices do not at all consider individual litigants or take into account the effect the Court's decisions may have on their lives."

This may seem a somewhat heartless attitude, but in reality it is the only way the system can work. Just as physicians cannot possibly become emotionally involved with their patients and still hope to practice good medicine, so Supreme Court justices cannot get involved with the litigants whose cases appear before them and still hope to practice good judicial law.

And there is one very beneficial result from this dispassionate approach. Hundreds of otherwise unknown and relatively unimportant people have been able to get their cases heard by the Supreme Court. Poor people, outcasts from society, men and women of all races, creeds, and colors have all had their day in court without the justices' paying any heed to the litigants' status or lack of status in society.

Dred Scott was one of those who probably never would have been heard if it had not been for the Supreme Court. He was just a poor old black man—in fact a slave—who was not called "Dred" at all, but "Sam," by several of his owners. Yet the name Dred Scott and the Dred Scott case were destined to go down in American history.

Not much is known about Dred Scott. He was probably born in Southampton County, Virginia, late in the eighteenth century, perhaps in 1795 or 1796. Because his parents were slaves owned by a man named Peter Blow, Dred Scott also grew up as a slave with Blow as his master.

In about 1830 Blow and his family moved to St. Louis, Missouri, taking Scott and several other slaves with them. A few years later Blow died and Scott was sold to an army physician, Dr. John Emerson, who was stationed at Jefferson Barracks, Missouri. When Emerson was transferred to Rock Island, Illinois, and later Fort Snelling, Minnesota (then part of the Wisconsin Territory), he took Scott with him. At this time, according to the Missouri Compromise of 1820, Missouri was a so-called slave state, while Illinois and Minnesota were part of a so-called free territory, where slavery was illegal.

The Missouri Compromise

Slavery first became truly a national issue in 1819. At that time Americans awakened to it, as Thomas Jefferson remarked, "as though a fire ball had rung in the night."

The alarm was sounded over Missouri's desire to become a state. To do so it had to draw up a constitution and submit it to the U.S. House of Representatives. Since slavery had been legal in Missouri up to this time, it was expected that it would continue to be legal under the state's proposed constitution. But abolitionist Congressman James Tallmadge of New York opposed this idea. He introduced an amendment to the Missouri statehood bill that would make it illegal to bring any more slaves into the state. Tallmadge's amendment also proposed that all children of slaves in Missouri should become free after they reached the age of twenty-five.

After fierce debate between the pro- and anti-slavery members of Congress, the House approved the amendment. But the Senate rejected it, and the debate continued to rage throughout the country until the next session of Congress.

By the time the next Congress met, Maine was also seeking statehood. At this session Congress agreed to let Maine enter the Union as a free state and Missouri as a slave state. At the same time Senator Jesse B. Thomas of Illinois proposed legislation that would prohibit any new slave states in the territory included in the Louisiana Purchase north of the 36 degree, 30 minute parallel of latitude. Since this line was to be the southern border of the proposed new state of Missouri, Missouri would be an exception to Thomas's proposal.

The Louisiana Purchase was the enormous tract of land purchased by the United States from France in 1803 during Thomas Jefferson's first term as president. The almost 900,000-square-mile territory was bought for $15 million. It included the area between the Rocky Mountains and the Mississippi River and extended from the Gulf of Mexico to the Canadian border. Eventually some fifteen states would be created out of the region, so the debate about whether or not slavery should be allowed in each of these new states was a vital one.

Senator Thomas's proposal for a dividing line between future slave and free states was accepted by the Congress. Later there were certain modifications of this so-called Missouri Compromise, and Missouri entered the Union as a slave state in February of 1821. Temporarily, the debate over slavery quieted down, but the Dred Scott case caused it to begin all over again.

Dred Scott Sues for His Freedom

In 1838 Dr. Emerson returned from Fort Snelling to Missouri, bringing with him Dred Scott, who by now had a family. While he had been in Minnesota, Scott had married, and he and his wife, Harriet, had two daughters, Eliza and Lizzie. Shortly after their return to Missouri Dr. Emerson died. The four members of the Scott family, still regarded as slaves, were left to Dr. Emerson's widow, Irene Emerson. But soon Mrs. Emerson moved to New York and left the Scott slaves in the possession of the sons of their original owner, Peter Blow. Peter Blow's sons were named Henry and Taylor.

Henry Blow was opposed to slavery, and it was probably at his prompting that Dred and Harriet Scott decided to sue for their freedom. The basis of their suit, filed in 1846, was that for a period of years Dred Scott had lived in a free territory, Illinois and Minnesota, and that his residence there should have made him a free man when he returned to the slave state of Missouri. If Scott was declared free, his wife and daughters would be free also.

The case dragged on for several years. While he waited, Scott was hired out to do odd jobs for a few dollars a month. At first a lower court decided in his favor, but then in 1852 the Missouri State Supreme Court reversed the lower court's decision. The matter did not rest there, however. By this time Scott's title as a slave had been transferred to John F. Sanford, the brother-in-law of Scott's earlier owner, Dr. John Emerson. In 1854 the case was once again renewed, this time in Missouri's Federal Circuit Court as *Scott* v. *Sandford*. (Sanford's name was misspelled in this instance.) But the Circuit

Dred Scott and his wife, Harriet. In 1857, the Supreme Court declared that Dred Scott, a slave, had no right to sue for his freedom in a Federal court. The controversy over this decision was one of the causes of the Civil War.

Court claimed it lacked jurisdiction in the case and passed the hot potato along to the U.S. Supreme Court in 1856.

At that time Roger B. Taney was Chief Justice. He and four others among the nine justices came from states where slavery was legal long before the Missouri Compromise. These five justices, comprising a majority of the Court, believed that despite the Missouri Compromise slaveholders could take their slaves wherever they wished and still retain their right to them as private property. Thus the majority of the Court was expected to rule that residence in a free state did not make a slave a free man or woman after he or she returned to a slave state.

But the minority members of the Court refused to go along with the majority and made it equally clear that they would issue strong dissenting opinions upholding the validity of the Missouri Compromise. Their dissenting opinions were expected to once again stir up public opinion regarding the slavery issue. Nevertheless, Taney prepared to render the Court's opinion on the matter and to do so in no uncertain terms as well as in great detail. This he believed would settle the matter once and for all. It did quite the opposite.

Taney's Controversial Decision in the Dred Scott Case

Taney had succeeded John Marshall as Chief Justice and while, like Marshall, he was a man of unassailable integrity, he had none of Marshall's tact, political astuteness, or judicial wisdom. In rendering the Supreme Court's majority opinion in the Dred Scott case on March 6, 1857, he declared flatly that, first of all, Scott had no right to bring suit in a Federal court because, according to the Constitution, since Scott was a slave he was not a citizen of the United States. The framers of the Constitution, Taney said, "agreed that Negroes were beings of an inferior order and altogether unfit to associate

Chief Justice Roger Brooke Taney presided over the Supreme Court
at the time of the Dred Scott case.

with the white race, either in social or political relations, and so far inferior that they had no rights which the white man was bound to respect." While Taney tried to make it clear that this was not necessarily what he himself believed but only what the framers of the Constitution believed, his intemperate words added fuel to the fire of the already blazing slavery controversy.

Secondly, Taney declared, even if Scott had a right to sue for his freedom he had not become a free man simply because he lived for a time in free territory, because the Missouri Compromise itself was unconstitutional. So, for the first time since *Marbury* v. *Madison,* the Supreme Court had declared an act of Congress unconstitutional, but this time in a far more major case.

Dred Scott was given his freedom (called manumission) by his master shortly after the Supreme Court rendered its decision against him, but he enjoyed his freedom for only about a year. During that time he worked as a hotel porter in St. Louis. He died on September 17, 1858, and his funeral was paid for by the Blow brothers.

But the Dred Scott case did not die with its subject. Partly because of the questions it raised, the tragic American Civil War was fought, and after the war the Thirteenth and Fourteenth Amendments were adopted. These both freed the slaves and made them citizens of the United States as well as of the states or territories in which they lived.

Lingering Effects of the Dred Scott Decision

Despite the passage of the Thirteenth and Fourteenth Amendments, however, the U.S. Supreme Court was a long time living down its decision in the Dred Scott case as announced by Chief Justice Taney. In today's parlance it would be said that "the Court shot itself in the foot." Perhaps a later

Chief Justice, Charles Evans Hughes, put it equally well when he said that the Court "suffered from a self-inflicted wound." He also called the ruling a "public calamity."

One important point should be remembered. Despite his lowly lot in life Dred Scott had been able to get his case heard by the nation's highest tribunal. And further, the innate fairness of the American people and their governmental institutions, of which the Supreme Court was just one, would eventually enable the "monumental indiscretion" committed by the Supreme Court to be reversed. Not only would there be Constitutional amendments to this effect, but also the Supreme Court itself would wash out the stain of the Dred Scott decision in the numerous civil rights cases brought before it in the twentieth century. Among the most important of these was *Brown* v. *Board of Education.*

4

The Bell Tolls for Linda Brown's Segregated School Days

The landmark Supreme Court decision in *Brown* v. *Board of Education* handed down in the mid-1950s apparently dealt strictly with racial segregation in the nation's public schools. But the decision had a ripple effect that resulted in major changes in race relations throughout American society—changes that are still going on today.

Technically the case began when Oliver Brown, a black minister in Topeka, Kansas, sued the local school board for the right to permit his daughter, Linda, to attend an all-white elementary school. Actually, however, the case began long before that—in fact, even before Linda Brown was born.

At the heart of the *Brown* v. *Board of Education* case was the "separate but equal" doctrine of education. This meant that it was legal for states to have separate public schools for white and black students so long as the quality of education was equal. At the time of the Brown decision some seventeen states, most of them in the South and Southwest, maintained racially separate systems of public education. The claim that the quality of education in the black schools was equal to that

in the white schools was a myth fostered by diehard segrega-
tionists. As a result, those who opposed segregation had long
fought to have officially sanctioned "separate but equal"
schools outlawed. The Brown case finally brought this matter
to a head.

The "separate but equal" doctrine grew out of so-called
Jim Crow laws passed by many Southern states after the Civil
War. The term *Jim Crow* for all blacks had been used by
white people since early in the nineteenth century. A white
entertainer, Thomas D. "Daddy" Rice, who wore blackface
makeup to perform his song and dance act, popularized the
term with a song he had picked up from the blacks. It went:

> Wheel about and turn about and do just so.
> Every time I wheel about I jump like Jim Crow.

Louisiana was one of the states that passed a number of
Jim Crow laws. One of them, passed on July 1, 1890, required
that railroads in the state carry blacks and whites in separate
cars. In 1892 a young black man named Homer Plessy decided
to test the validity of this law. Boarding a train on the East
Louisiana Railroad, Plessy took a seat in a white coach. When
asked to move to a Jim Crow coach, Plessy refused to do so.
He was promptly arrested and later brought into a New Orleans court and charged with violating the Jim Crow railroad
car law.

In court Plessy was represented by Albion W. Tourgée, a
lawyer of French Huguenot parentage and a staunch desegre-
gationist. The judge before whom Plessy appeared, John H.
Ferguson, ruled that Plessy was guilty, whereupon Tourgée
appealed the *Plessy* v. *Ferguson* case to the state supreme
court. When the case against Plessy was upheld, Tourgée appealed it to the U.S. Supreme Court.

This case, like most others, dragged on for many years, but finally, on May 18, 1896, the Court handed down its decision. It also ruled against Plessy, upholding Judge Ferguson's original decision on the grounds that the "separate but equal" doctrine was legal. In supporting the decision in *Plessy* v. *Ferguson,* the Court went even a step further. It pointed out that segregation on public transportation was no different from segregation in the public schools, where "separate but equal" laws had been in effect and upheld by the courts for many years.

The *Plessy* v. *Ferguson* ruling by the Supreme Court, despite the fact that it was in clear violation of the Fourteenth Amendment to the Constitution, thus remained the law of the land until Linda Brown's father decided that his daughter should be allowed to attend a white school. At this point the modern Civil Rights Movement truly began.

Thurgood Marshall Champions Linda Brown's Case

From the time it was founded in 1909 the National Association for the Advancement of Colored People (NAACP) led the fight for racial equality throughout the United States. One of the NAACP's most important leaders in the fight was a black lawyer named Thurgood Marshall, who has sometimes been called "Mr. Civil Rights."

Born in Baltimore, Maryland, just a year before the NAACP was founded, Marshall was destined to become in 1967 the first black U.S. Supreme Court justice. Before that, however, Marshall had received his law degree from Howard University in Washington, D.C., and had become the legal counsel for the NAACP in 1938.

Marshall concentrated his racial equality efforts by attacking segregation in the nation's public schools, particularly in the South and Southwest. His efforts were successful in forcing state universities in Missouri, Oklahoma, and Texas to accept black students. But he had no success when he attempted to persuade public schools below the college and university level to gradually allow black students to attend white schools. Actually, many black leaders were as opposed to this process of "gradualism" as were the southern school board members. Finally, Marshall decided to wage a full-scale frontal attack in the nation's courts against segregated public schools.

Marshall began his campaign by bringing suits against various local elementary school boards in several states. The suits charged not only that the quality of education in the black schools was inferior to that in the white schools but also that these so-called separate but equal schools were unconstitutional under the Fourteenth Amendment. One of the suits that Marshall launched was that of *Linda Brown* v. *the Board of Education of Topeka, Kansas.*

But in response to each of these suits local courts and state supreme courts held that the *Plessy* v. *Ferguson* doctrine of "separate but equal" was still valid. Marshall then appealed the cases to the U.S. Supreme Court.

Although the Court received legal briefs on all of the cases, the central one was *Brown* v. *Board of Education.* In this brief Marshall said:

> The evidence makes it clear that it was the intent of the proponents of the Fourteenth Amendment that it could of its own force prohibit all state action based upon race or color and all segregation in public education. The "separate but equal" rule of *Plessy* v. *Ferguson* was conceived in error and should be reversed forthwith. Moreover, any delay in executing the judgment of the Court would involve insurmountable difficulties, so that the plaintiff in question should be admitted at once without distinctions of race or color to the school of her choice.

With his brief Marshall presented an enormous amount of evidence that his staff, aided by many volunteer historians, had compiled to make clear the damage done to blacks as a result of the "separate but equal" rule. The Court took many weeks to study this material, but finally on May 17, 1954, it rendered its unanimous decision. The decision was read by Chief Justice Earl Warren. In part Warren said:

> School segregation by state law causes a feeling of inferiority in black children that inflicts damage to their hearts and minds that may never be undone. Public school segregation by state law, therefore, violates the equal protection clause of the Fourteenth Amendment. . . . The old Plessy "separate but equal" rule is herewith formally overruled.

Unquestionably Thurgood Marshall and the Civil Rights cause had won a landmark victory. But the positive results of the victory were slow in coming. For one thing the desegregation of the nation's public schools was not immediately accomplished because the Court also ordered that it be carried out "with all deliberate speed." This was an immediate signal for reluctant school boards to sit on their hands until they were forced by local federal courts to take action.

And other Jim Crow laws did not collapse without a fierce struggle. Segregation in buses and restaurants and at the voting booth had to be challenged with boycotts, sit-ins, marches, and other demonstrations. But within the next fifteen years after the Linda Brown decision the principles of that decision were written into new laws prohibiting discrimination in public accommodations, employment, housing, and numerous other areas throughout American society.

Perhaps the most important developments of all growing out of the Brown case were the 1964 Civil Rights Act and the

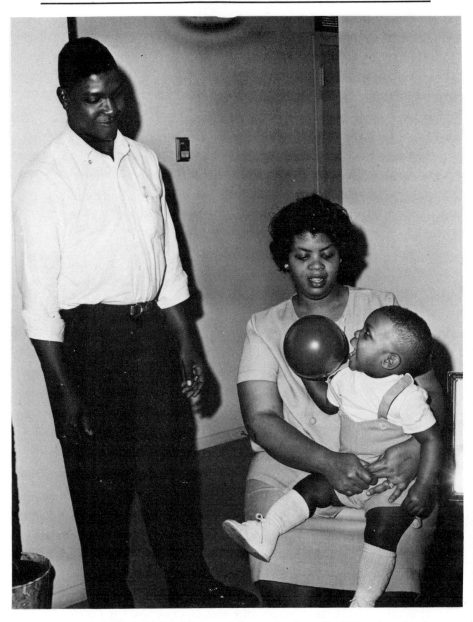

The modern Civil Rights Movement began in the mid-1950s when Linda Brown's father sued the local school board for the right of his daughter to attend an all-white school. Linda is shown here in 1964 with her husband, Charles F. Smith, and son, Chuckie.

1965 Voting Rights Act. The former made the U.S Justice Department responsible for the enforcement of school desegregation programs. The latter finally secured the right of all black adults to vote in local and national elections, which has resulted in blacks' winning an ever-increasing number of political offices and gaining political awareness and strength.

Continuing Civil Rights Conflict

But all has not been sweetness and light in regard to school desegregation or other kinds of affirmative action in the Civil Rights struggle. Certain cities in both the North and South have resorted to extreme measures to avoid the observance of racial equality. White students have left public schools and enrolled in segregated private schools. For many years the citizens of Boston, Massachusetts, have been involved in serious controversy over the matter of busing students from one area school to another to promote racial equality. Similar pro- and anti-busing battles have also gone on elsewhere. The city of Cairo, Illinois, virtually destroyed itself in the fight against desegregation, going to such extreme lengths as to fill in a municipal swimming pool with cement to prevent blacks from using it.

Perhaps the most interesting reaction to the affirmative action efforts has been a backlash in which whites have claimed that since the Brown decision they have been the victims of reverse discrimination. In the late 1970s a young white man, Alan Bakke, who wanted to become a physician, was refused admittance to a California school on the grounds that the quota for white students had already been filled. Bakke promptly entered a suit based on the equal protection clause of the Fourteenth Amendment, claiming reverse discrimination. Eventually Bakke's case reached the U.S. Supreme Court.

5

The Bakke Case

In an attempt to make up for the many years of discrimination against blacks, affirmative action on behalf of minority groups became a powerful movement throughout much of American society following the Supreme Court decision in the Linda Brown case. For example, a system of employment quotas, reserving a certain number of job openings for members of minority groups, began to be widely used by businesses and local, state, and federal government departments.

In Chicago, a quota system was established on the basis of the ratio between blacks and whites in the city's total population. Once this ratio—based on census returns—was established, a certain percentage of new employees in such organizations as the police and fire departments had to be white and a certain percentage had to be black. Similar systems were established elsewhere throughout the country.

At first many businesses went along somewhat reluctantly with this kind of affirmative action in hiring new employees. But with the passage of the Civil Rights Act of 1964 it became illegal for businesses to continue discriminatory employment practices. Title VII of the Civil Rights Act bars all job discrimination on the basis of race, sex, religion, or national origin.

Gradually the quota system also began to move into the field of higher education. This was not merely out of kindness and compassion but because Title VI of the Civil Rights Act also forbids discrimination in any program or activity receiving federal financial assistance. Most colleges and universities, of course, receive such assistance. In fact in many advanced educational institutions federal funds make up a major portion of the budget.

One of the places where quotas were first established in the education field was in the acceptance of students into medical schools. Before the 1960s American medical schools were almost wholly filled with white students. To remedy this situation many programs were begun in which each beginning medical school class would be required to have in it a certain percentage of minority members. A leader in this movement was the University of California's medical facility at its Davis campus.

The Davis campus medical school first opened in 1968. Although only about 3 percent of its first classes were blacks, Asian-Americans, and Hispanics, by 1972 sixteen out of one hundred first-year medical students were minority or so-called disadvantaged students. This record gave every promise of improving, and the University of California was widely hailed as a leader in progressive affirmative action.

But there was one point of contention: some minority applicants with lower scholastic grades than white applicants were being accepted into the Davis medical school simply to fill the minority quota. Since competition to get into medical schools has always been fierce, many white applicants objected to this additional barrier. Nothing much was done about it, however, until a white applicant named Allan Bakke came along.

Actually the medical school situation was not unlike the problem encountered by numerous urban police and fire departments where the same kind of favoritism was being shown to members of minority groups. In order to fill racial and ethnic employment quotas as well as to promote already-employed minority members, blacks and Hispanics with lower test scores than whites were not infrequently the ones hired or promoted.

Such apparent favoritism was justified, according to affirmative action spokespersons, on the grounds that whites had long discriminated against minorities, especially blacks, and this was simply the only way for blacks to catch up. Some whites, on the other hand, insisted that the quality of such organizations as police and fire departments was being weakened by the failure to select the best candidate as indicated by test scores. Blacks claimed that the qualification tests were devised by whites and thus were unfair and discriminatory in themselves. Had the tests been devised by blacks, they claimed, blacks would have outscored whites. Blacks and Hispanics also pointed out that since the minority populations of many urban areas were equal to if not greater than the white population it was only fair that the emergency service organizations be equally racially representative.

The debate has continued to the present day, although in 1984 the Supreme Court made a ruling that somewhat clarified the affirmative action problem in regard to hiring and firing of city employees on a quota basis.

The Memphis Firefighters' Dispute
This ruling resulted from a suit brought by the Memphis, Tennessee, Fire Department Union to prevent the firing of white firefighters with greater seniority than blacks hired under an affirmative action program. The situation developed when the city of Memphis was caught in an economic crunch and had to cut back on the size of its fire department. Affirmative action

leaders insisted that in order to maintain the required number of black firefighters under the quota system white firefighters would have to be laid off first. But the firefighters' union insisted that in all previous personnel reductions the rule of "last hired, first fired" had applied and it should continue to apply in this case. Thus, since all of the most recently hired firefighters were blacks, only blacks would be fired and this would unbalance the quota agreement. The result was a suit that traveled all the way to the Supreme Court.

In June of 1984 the Court upheld the firefighters' union practice of "last hired, first fired." In doing so the high court said that the 1964 Civil Rights Act "protects the seniority of 'innocent employees' when there has been no finding of intentional discrimination. It is inappropriate to deny an innocent employee the benefits of his seniority in order to provide a remedy. . . . An individual is not automatically entitled to have a nonminority employee laid off to make room for him."

There was immediate objection to this Supreme Court decision by the NAACP and various women's groups. They claimed that "the ruling placed the burden of adverse economic conditions even more heavily on minorities and women, who have only recently entered many sectors of the work force previously closed to them."

But the ruling stood, although the debate about its precise meaning in the overall minorities versus whites employment picture has continued.

Court observers have pointed out that the Memphis decision was probably based in part at least on the somewhat similar earlier ruling in the Bakke case, which was the first such reverse discrimination decision made by the high tribunal.

Allan Bakke's Reverse Discrimination Claim

Allan Bakke was a late bloomer as far as his medical career was concerned. He was already thirty-two when he decided he wanted to become a doctor. But he was also already a high achiever in other fields. He had graduated with honors in mechanical engineering from the University of Minnesota and had served with distinction with the United States Marines in Vietnam during the Vietnam War. It was, in fact, during his stint in Vietnam that he became interested in the study of medicine.

After the war Bakke earned his master's degree in engineering at Stanford University, where he also took premedical courses in biology and chemistry. To help support himself at Stanford, Bakke worked nights in the emergency room of a hospital in Mountain View, California. It was there that he decided to become a doctor, and he took all of the required premed courses. In 1972 Bakke applied for entrance into a dozen different medical schools, including the one at the University of California's Davis campus.

In the beginning Bakke believed that only his age might prevent him from being accepted as a medical student. He was certain he could overcome this apparent disadvantage by persuading admissions interviewers of his dedication to medicine. He was by now obsessed with the idea of becoming a doctor. His grades, he believed, were more than adequate.

But, much to his surprise and disappointment, Bakke was refused admission to all of the medical schools where he applied, including the one at Davis. Following these rejections, Bakke wrote the Davis admissions director requesting that he be put on a standby basis or allowed to take medical courses as a special student. He received no reply to his letter.

Obviously the Davis authorities had not reckoned with Allan Bakke's determination. Soon they received another letter from him, which read in part:

> I feel compelled to pursue a further course of action. Applicants chosen to be our doctors should be those presenting the best qualifications, both academic and personal. I am convinced a significant fraction is judged by a separate criterion. I am referring to quotas, open or

covert, for racial minorities. I realize that the rationale
for these quotas is that they attempt to atone for past
discrimination. But instituting a new racial bias in favor
of minorities is not a just solution.

In fact, I believe that admissions quotas based on
race are illegal. For this reason I am inquiring of friends
about the possibility of formally challenging these quotas
through the courts. My main reason would be to secure
admission for myself—I consider the goal worth fighting
for in every legal or ethical way.

The response Bakke received to this letter was a sugges-
tion that he reapply for admission to Davis in the fall of 1974.
He did so but was again rejected. He then sought a lawyer to
represent him. The man he selected was Reynold Colvin of
San Francisco, who had strong opinions about reverse discrimination.

Colvin first tried to get Bakke admitted to Davis. When
this effort failed, he had Bakke file suit against the school. In
time the suit reached the California Supreme Court, which
ruled in Bakke's favor in September 1976. In its ruling the
court said: "We conclude that the program, as administered
by the University, violates the constitutional rights of nonminority applicants, because if affords preference on the basis
of race to persons who, by the University's own standards, are
not as qualified for the study of medicine as nonminority applicants denied admission."

The decision was soon appealed to the United States Supreme Court. Representing the University of California in
this appeal was Archibald Cox. A professor of law at Harvard
University, Cox had gained fame during the Watergate hearings, which resulted in Richard Nixon's being the first president of the United States to resign.

Cox had appeared before the Supreme Court many times,
but this was Colvin's baptism before the high tribunal. The

Warren Burger was Chief Justice at the time of the Allan Bakke case. Bakke challenged the quota system under which a certain number of school admissions are reserved for minority students. His suit claimed reverse discrimination.

Court hearings were held on October 12, 1977. Bakke had been trying to become a medical student for five years, and now he was thirty-seven years old.

Cox's arguments were based on the legitimacy of the University of California's quota system as a simple method of redressing the long years of racial discrimination against minorities.

Colvin argued that it was his client, Allan Bakke, who had been discriminated against.

There were numerous sharp exchanges between various members of the Court and the two lawyers, and it soon became clear that the justices themselves were divided on the issues involved. Clearly the debate centered around the equal protection clause of the Fourteenth Amendment and Title 6 of the Civil Rights Act. But how the justices would resolve the debate was not clear.

Once again the justices were a long time in deciding. They did not do so, in fact, until nine months after the original hearings. Then, when the ruling was announced on June 28, 1978, it turned out to be a split decision! Four justices lined up on one side, four on the other, and one in the middle.

The Supreme Court decision did rule, however, that Davis's special admissions program was illegal because the racial quota was invalid and that Bakke must be admitted to the school. On the other hand, it left the door open to affirmative action programs, implying that they were a "good thing" but should not be the determining factor in a school admissions program.

Although the media and the public were generally confused by the scattershot decision in the Bakke case, Allan Bakke got what he was after. He entered the Davis medical school in the fall of 1978 and concentrated on his studies, avoiding all publicity for four straight years. He was awarded the degree of Doctor of Medicine in 1981 and went on to study anesthesiology. Then he returned to Minnesota to become an anesthesiologist at the famed Mayo Clinic in Rochester.

As Fred W. Friendly and Martha J.H. Elliott have pointed out in *The Constitution, That Delicate Balance:* "Allan Bakke made his point in the highest court in the land, but history will render the final verdict in this classic test of rights under the 14th Amendment."

6

The Miranda Case and Its Aftermath

Of all the cases decided by the Supreme Court some of the most dramatic and important in their impact upon American society have been those involving criminal justice. And among these none has been more controversial than the Miranda case.

Ernesto Miranda was sentenced to a prison term of twenty to thirty years in the mid-1960s for kidnaping and raping a Phoenix, Arizona, woman. After Miranda was sent to prison, his lawyer appealed the case on the grounds that before and during his trial Miranda had been forced to incriminate himself, which is a violation of the Fifth Amendment of the Bill of Rights.

The basis for the self-incrimination charge was the fact that following his arrest Miranda had been forced to undergo a lengthy police interrogation and had signed a confession that was used to convict him. His lawyer claimed that not only had the confession been forced but at no time had the police ever warned Miranda that he did not have to speak if he did not want to and that anything he might volunteer to say could be used against him at his trial. This latter point also was un-constitutional, his lawyer insisted—and the Supreme Court agreed with him.

On June 16, 1966, the Supreme Court ordered a retrial for Miranda. In announcing the Court's majority opinion Chief Justice Earl Warren said:

> Unless other fully effective means are devised to in-form accused persons of their right of silence and to as-sure a continuous opportunity to exercise it, the following measures are required: Prior to any question-ing, the person must be warned that he has the right to remain silent, that any statement he does make may be used as evidence against him, and that he has a right to the presence of an attorney, either retained or ap-pointed. The defendant may waive effectuation of these rights, provided the waiver is made voluntarily, know-ingly, and intelligently. If, however, he indicates in any manner and at any stage of the process that he wishes to consult with an attorney before speaking, there can be no questioning. Likewise, if the individual is alone and indi-cates in any manner that he does not wish to be interro-gated, the police may not question him. The mere fact that he may have answered some questions or volun-teered some statements on his own does not deprive him of the right to refrain from answering any further inqui-ries until he has consulted with an attorney and there-after consents to be questioned.

At his second trial Miranda was again convicted and re-mained in prison until he was paroled at the end of 1972. He then got a job as a deliveryman and seemed to be following a quiet, law-abiding life as a parolee. Early in 1976, however, Miranda, who was then just thirty-four, got into a fight in a Phoenix bar over a poker game and was stabbed to death. His assailant escaped.

Ernesto Miranda at the time of his trial for kidnapping and rape. After conviction, Miranda sued, saying he had never been told of his right to silence when questioned by the police. The Supreme Court decision led to the Miranda rule in which an apprehended person must be advised of his rights.

But the controversy over the Supreme Court's ruling in his case did not die with Miranda. Police and law enforcement agencies across the land claimed that the Miranda decision gave undue protection to suspects and made investigations and convictions much more difficult than ever before. Criminals were being pampered, law enforcement officers claimed, while their victims were being ignored.

Partly because of these complaints and partly because of a demand by the public for more law and order, the Supreme Court as well as other federal courts began to modify the Miranda rule and other similar rulings. Court observers pointed out that under the new Chief Justice, Warren Burger, the Supreme Court's decisions had become more conservative, following the pattern of the strongly conservative Ronald Reagan administration.

Encounter in a Supermarket

In September of 1980 a woman told two New York police officers on patrol that she had just been raped by a man who had fled into a nearby supermarket. The officers entered the store and saw a man resembling the description given them by the woman. As soon as the suspect saw the policemen he ran toward a rear door, but he was stopped at gunpoint by one of the officers.

The suspect was named Benjamin Quarles. The police officers immediately handcuffed Quarles and searched him. They found he was wearing an empty shoulder holster. Normally this would have been the point at which one of the officers read Quarles his Miranda rights. Instead, he asked Quarles where the gun was. The suspect pointed to a pile of empty cardboard boxes and said, "The gun's over there."

The police officer searched the pile of boxes and found a loaded .38 caliber revolver. He then arrested Quarles and read him his rights.

When Quarles was brought to trial a judge excluded much of the evidence against him on the grounds that the suspect had not been given the Miranda warning soon enough. But when the Supreme Court finally heard the appeal and rendered its decision in June of 1984, the Court ruled in favor of the arresting officers on the grounds that when confronted by threats to public safety police are not required to immediately read suspects in criminal cases their Miranda rights. The Court also ruled that any incriminating statements made by such suspects in similar circumstances before their rights are read to them can be used in evidence.

In support of the majority opinion Justice William Rehnquist said, "The police in this case were faced with the immediate necessity of ascertaining the whereabouts of a gun which they had every reason to believe the suspect had just removed from his holster and discarded in the supermarket.

"So long as the gun was concealed somewhere in the supermarket, with its actual whereabouts unknown, it obviously posed more than one danger to the public safety. An accomplice might make use of it; a customer or employee might later come upon it."

Rehnquist added that if the police had been required to recite the Miranda warnings beforehand, Quarles might not have responded and the concealment of the gun in a public area could have caused "further danger to the public."

A Second Miranda Exception

Nine months after its decision in the Quarles supermarket case the Supreme Court created a second exception to the controversial Miranda rule. This occurred following the arrest of eighteen-year-old Michael James Elstad in Salem, Oregon, as a suspect in the $150,000 burglary of a neighbor's home.

Salem police, armed with a warrant, questioned teenager Elstad in his parents' home. Without telling him of his rights the police asked Elstad about the burglary, and the youth admitted, "Yes, I was there." He was then arrested and taken to the local police headquarters, where he was read his rights. Elstad again confessed, this time in writing.

Elstad was convicted of the burglary, but a state appeals court reversed the conviction on the grounds that the first confession, illegally obtained, influenced the making of the second and rendered it inadmissible in court. In other words, as the court said, after Elstad's first statement, "the cat was sufficiently out of the bag" so that he confessed more readily a second time.

When the state court's decision was appealed to the Supreme Court, the majority of the justices did not go along with this kind of "psychological analysis" of the twin confessions. On March 14, 1985, the Supreme Court ruled that "a simple failure by police to administer the warning unaccompanied by any actual coercion did not taint the second confession so that police would be barred from using it at trial."

Lower courts, the Court ruling continued, "should avoid a rigid rule in Miranda cases and look at the circumstances in deciding whether a confession is voluntary and may be used in trial."

In commenting on the Elstad confession decision Justice Sandra Day O'Connor insisted that in making it, "the Court in no way retreats from the . . . rule of Miranda." But there were many who felt otherwise. These included several Supreme Court justices as well as numerous media commentators throughout the country.

Justices William J. Brennan, Jr., and Thurgood Marshall accused the majority of the Court of "delivering a potentially crippling blow to Miranda and the ability of the courts to safeguard the rights of persons accused of crime." Brennan added that the Court was engaged "in a studied campaign to strip the Miranda decision piecemeal."

Typical of many newspaper editorial comments was that made by the Chicago *Tribune* on March 9, 1985. Under the title "Throwing Mud on Miranda," the *Tribune* editorial read in part:

> . . . the best thing about the Miranda rule has always been its clarity. Sure, a police officer could bollix up an interrogation and run afoul of the rule, but it wasn't easy. If police had a suspect in custody, they simply had to read him his rights before asking the first question. And if they had any doubts about whether they had custody of the suspect, they could protect their case by hauling the Miranda card out of a pocket and reciting the litany of rights.
>
> Now the Supreme Court has gone and muddied up the law, making it suddenly unclear when a police officer must read a suspect his rights. . . . In many circumstances, of course, it will still make sense for police to read the rights immediately. But now there will be a temptation to try to shave the rule as much as possible— in hopes that if the suspect confessed once in ignorance of his rights, he might be confused enough to think it makes no difference to confess again after the ritual reading of the words.
>
> Just how much of this will the Supreme Court tolerate? . . . the problem with this new opinion is that for no good reason, except perhaps to uphold the burglary conviction of a single man, the Court has rendered ambiguous what had been certain.

Despite the numerous breastbeatings about weakening the Miranda rule, the man and woman in the street generally seemed to approve any and all efforts to rid their streets of crime, even if it did perhaps mean pampering the victims for a change rather than the criminals. Consequently, the debate over the Miranda rule and others of a similar nature would doubtless continue to rage for many months and years to come.

7

Gideon's Trumpet Is Heard in the Land

A modest granite gravestone at Mount Olivet Cemetery near Hannibal, Missouri, bears a name that is unfamiliar to most people. It is Clarence Earl Gideon, who died a pauper in 1972.

Also inscribed on the stone are the words, "Each era finds an improvement in law for the benefit of mankind." These were the words that Gideon himself wrote to his lawyer, Abe Fortas, who once represented Gideon before the United States Supreme Court.

Who was this man Gideon? On the face of it, just a petty thief who died of tuberculosis at age sixty-two. But actually he was much more than that. He was the stubborn, driving force behind a Supreme Court case that firmly established the Constitutional right of a poor criminal defendant to be given free legal counsel.

Gideon's alleged crime was breaking into a Panama City, Florida, pool hall. Although he had only an eighth grade education, Gideon was forced to defend himself at his trial because he could not afford to hire a lawyer. He was promptly sentenced to serve a five-year term in the Florida State Prison at Raiford, Florida. As soon as he got to prison Gideon began to consider how to appeal the injustice he felt had been done to him. Finally he sat down and wrote a letter in longhand, in pencil, on prison stationery. The letter was addressed to the United States Supreme Court.

As United States Attorney General Robert F. Kennedy later said, "If an obscure Florida convict named Clarence Earl Gideon had not sat down in his prison cell to write a letter to the Supreme Court, the vast machinery of American law would have gone on functioning undisturbed. But Gideon did write that letter, the Court did look into his case, and the whole course of American legal history has been changed."

School Dropout and Wanderer

If ten students in the Hannibal, Missouri, public schools during the 1920s had been selected as the least likely to succeed, young Clarence Earl Gideon probably would have headed the list. And by the time he was in his fifties he would have lived up to that prophecy. In and out of jails most of his life, he had served time for four felonies before his Panama City conviction, and he bore the physical marks to prove his seemingly wasted life. He looked frail and old beyond his years, both his voice and his hands trembled, and his hair was white. But his barren life had not extinguished the gemlike flame of fierce independence that had burned in Gideon from the time he was a boy.

Clarence Earl Gideon was born in Hannibal on August 30, 1910, the only child of Charles and Virginia Gideon. His father died when young Gideon was three, and his mother remarried two years later. His stepfather, Marion Anderson, a widower and a factory worker with a son and daughter by his earlier marriage, was a devout member of the Baptist

Church and a strict disciplinarian. Young Gideon did not get along with him and ran away from home when he was fourteen.

The teenage boy led the life of a hobo and wanderer for a year before returning to Missouri. He arrived in his home state in midwinter, and to keep from freezing to death he broke into a country store and stole some clothing. The next day he was caught wearing the stolen clothing, and a short time later he was tried in juvenile court and sentenced to three years in the state juvenile reformatory.

Paroled after a year, Gideon succeeded in getting a job in a shoe factory, earning two dollars a day. By the time he was in his late teens he was making twenty-five dollars a week and decided to get married. In 1928, when he was just eighteen, he lost his job. He committed several robberies and burglaries to support his wife and himself. Again he was caught, and this time he was sentenced to serve ten years in the Missouri State Prison. He was paroled in three years.

Gideon got out of prison at a bad time. The country was in the midst of its greatest economic depression, during the 1930s, and there were few jobs to be had, even for a law-abiding citizen. He did work briefly in a shoe factory, but when that job ran out Gideon again resorted to burglary. This time he broke into a government armory. When caught he was tried in a federal court and sentenced to three years in the federal prison at Fort Leavenworth, Kansas.

Given a conditional release in 1937 after serving about two years, Gideon again tried unsuccessfully to get a job and was refused government welfare aid because of his prison record. He then resumed his life as a wanderer and petty criminal.

For the next quarter of a century Gideon lived in the backwaters of American society and could clearly be regarded as one of life's outcasts. His wanderings took him from Missouri to Texas to Louisiana and finally to Panama City, Florida. Along the way he worked as a railroad brakeman, short-order cook, gambler, automobile mechanic, and tavern operator. Also along the way there were numerous burglary arrests and brief jail sentences.

In 1953 Gideon's health broke down, and he was hospitalized in the Public Health Service Sanitarium in New Orleans. He was treated for tuberculosis until his release in 1954. Following his release, he returned to Missouri, where he met and married his second wife—what happened to his first wife is not clear—and the couple moved to Orange, Texas. There Gideon ran a pool hall and tavern and met Ruth Babineaux, the woman who was to become his third wife and mother of his children. A divorcee and mother of three children by her first husband, she worked for Gideon at his tavern. Soon after they met, Gideon divorced his second wife and married Mrs. Babineaux. Together they took custody of her three children, two sons and a daughter.

Then the Gideons had two sons and a daughter of their own. Gideon was harder-pressed than ever to make a living. Eventually he abandoned the tavern business and moved his family to Panama City, Florida, where he resumed his life as a professional gambler. Again this illegal occupation landed him in jail for brief periods. Between jail terms he also tried to earn a living as an automobile mechanic, but he was none too successful.

Gideon tried to rear his children correctly. He and his wife joined a Baptist Church at Cedar Grove, Florida, and the church people took an active interest in the Gideon children. But once again hard luck, the blind fates, or whatever it was that had plagued Gideon all of his life intervened. His tuberculosis returned, and he was hospitalized at Tallahassee.

While Gideon was in the hospital the Baptist Church members did their best to take care of his family, but soon the Department of Public Welfare had to step in and take charge of the children. Eventually Gideon had to undergo surgery to have part of one of his diseased lungs removed. By the time he had fully recovered, his wife had deserted him, turning the children over to the Public Welfare authorities.

Upon his discharge from the Tallahassee hospital Gideon made valiant efforts to earn enough money to regain custody of his children. He worked both as an automobile mechanic and gambler but could never quite manage to clear the amount of money needed for this purpose. It was while he was in the midst of his custody struggle that Gideon was suddenly arrested, tried, and sentenced to prison for breaking into the pool hall in Panama City—the event that was to lead to the landmark Supreme Court decision regarding free legal counsel for poor criminal defendants.

The Panama City Pool Hall Burglary

At about midnight on June 2, 1961, Ira Strickland, Jr., operator of the Bay Harbor Poolroom, a tavern in Panama City, closed and locked his place of business for the night. The next morning when Strickland returned at 8 o'clock to reopen the tavern, the local sheriff was waiting to tell him that the place had been broken into. A window had been smashed, and the cigarette machine and juke box had apparently been tampered with and some coins were stolen. Strickland quickly inspected the premises and said that money from the two machines had indeed been stolen as well as a small amount of beer and wine.

There apparently was one witness to the burglary. A man named Henry Cook, of Panama City, said that he had been standing outside the Bay Harbor Poolroom early that morning and had seen Gideon, whom he knew, inside. A short time later, Cook said, Gideon came out carrying a bottle of wine, made a telephone call from a nearby pay telephone, and in a little while was picked up by a taxi, which he had evidently called.

Cook, however, did not first report the break-in. It was discovered by a police officer on patrol, Henry Berryhill, Jr., who found the front door of the tavern open. Cook, still at the scene, told Berryhill that he had seen Gideon leaving the building.

A short time later Gideon was arrested and charged with breaking and entering the Bay Harbor Poolroom with intent to commit a felony. He was tried on August 4, 1961, in a Florida Circuit Court, before Judge Robert L. McCrary, Jr., and a jury of six men.

At his trial Gideon insisted that he did not break into the tavern, that indeed he would not have had to because he had a key to the place. The reason he had a key was because, he claimed, he worked there part-time for Strickland. He also strongly implied that he had been falsely accused of the crime because of his past record and because of his reputation as a gambler.

But the most important point made by Gideon before Judge McCrary was in his statement that he was too poor to afford a lawyer and his request that a lawyer be appointed for him by the court.

Judge McCrary replied, "I am sorry, but I cannot appoint counsel to represent you in this case. Under the laws of the State of Florida the only time the court can appoint counsel to represent a defendant is when that person is charged with a capital offense. I am sorry, but I will have to deny your request to appoint counsel to defend you in this case."

Gideon insisted: "The United States Supreme Court says I am entitled to be represented by counsel."

Despite Gideon's objections, the trial was held, and a few hours later the defendant was found guilty and sentenced to five years in prison.

The *Betts* v. *Brady* Precedent

Actually Gideon was wrong in his claim, and the reason he was wrong was because of an earlier precedent established in a Supreme Court case known as *Betts* v. *Brady*.

Smith Betts was a farm worker in Maryland who was charged with robbery. Too poor to hire a lawyer, Betts asked the court to appoint one for him. Betts was told, just as Gideon later would be, that Maryland appointed lawyers only for poor defendants accused of such capital crimes as murder and rape. Betts was tried, found guilty, and sentenced to eight years in prison.

Betts appealed his case on the grounds that the failure to provide him with counsel violated his constitutional rights. But in 1942 the Supreme Court ruled against Betts, stating that "in the great majority of states appointment of counsel is not a fundamental right essential to a fair trial." While most of the states did require the appointment of lawyers for poor defendants in capital cases, the Supreme Court pointed out that to rule in favor of Betts would eventually "require the appointment of counsel in traffic courts" and other relatively minor cases.

Since 1942 the *Betts* v. *Brady* decision had been accepted as a basic rule of law in judicial proceedings throughout the United States. In fact, in 1947 Justice Felix Frankfurter went a step further in reinforcing the policy by stating that to provide free counsel for all poor defendants would threaten the "opening wide of prison doors of the land."

Nevertheless, there had been a groundswell of feeling against the *Betts* v. *Brady* decision by numerous justices, not only in the Supreme Court but also in lower federal courts. A number of authorities thought that just as *Plessy* v. *Ferguson* had legally denied blacks their constitutional rights for many years, so *Betts* v. *Brady* was denying basic constitutional rights to thousands of American citizens just because they were poor. As a result, there had grown up among most members of the Supreme Court a conviction that sooner or later they would have to face up to a true test of the Betts decision that might well result in its reversal.

When Gideon's penciled, longhand letter reached the Supreme Court the time was ripe for testing *Betts* v. *Brady*. But in his letter Gideon made no reference at all to that time-honored ruling. He did not claim any special circumstances that might have applied in his case, nor did he pretend that he had been tried for a capital crime. What Gideon's letter said was plain and simple: "I requested the court to appoint me [an] attorney, and the court refused." This, the letter continued, was a violation of the Fourteenth Amendment, which states that "no state shall deprive any person of life, liberty, or property without the process of law."

How Gideon's Case Came Before the Court

Each year the United States Supreme Court hears fewer than 200 cases, a relatively small number out of the more than twelve million cases tried annually in American courts. Of these, several hundred thousand are appealed, but only several thousand litigants seek to have their cases reviewed by the U.S. Supreme Court. Of these, between 140 and 170 are actually heard by the nation's highest tribunal.

Among the Supreme Court's provisions for hearings before the Court is a federal law that allows poor people or paupers to have their cases considered without following all of the strictly legal procedures and without paying the regular costs. This procedure is called *in forma pauperis,* or in the manner of a pauper. Under it, for example, a litigant may file just one copy of a petition to appear before the Court rather than the forty or fifty usually required. Similar savings and shortcuts are allowed in all other procedural areas.

Gideon's petition was filed *in forma pauperis.* It included a copy of a written request to the Florida Supreme Court that he be freed, on the grounds that he had originally been illegally imprisoned. This is called a *writ of habeas corpus.* It was legally necessary for Gideon to have filed such a writ if the U.S. Supreme Court was to consider hearing his case. From the fact that Gideon had done so and from other indications—the use of certain required legal language, for instance—it was clear that if Gideon had accomplished nothing else during his frequent stays in jail he had occupied his time well in various prison libraries. There was no doubt that Gideon had become something of a jailhouse lawyer and knew what he was about in his application for a hearing.

But just because Gideon's request had arrived at the Supreme Court building in Washington, had been checked by a law clerk to see if it met the limited legal requirements, and then had been filed along with hundreds of other *in forma pauperis* requests there was no assurance whatsoever that any further action would be taken on it. In fact less than 5 percent of all such requests are ever considered for hearing by the Court.

In this particular instance, and perhaps for the first time in his life, Gideon was lucky. His timing was right. All of the justices had been growing more and more sensitive about the earlier Court's Betts decision, and they and their law clerks had their eyes out for any new case that might justify a *Betts*

v. *Brady* reversal. Even though the Betts case was not referred to in Gideon's pauper's request for a hearing the request looked as though it might be just the one they had been looking for.

As a result, two things happened. The Supreme Court asked the State of Florida for a response to Gideon's *habeas corpus* request, and a lawyer was appointed to represent Gideon before the high tribunal.

As was to be expected, the Florida State authorities simply replied that Gideon's *habeas corpus* request had not been granted on the grounds that Gideon had not originally been entitled to have a free trial lawyer on the basis of the 1942 *Betts* v. *Brady* ruling. His offense was not a capital crime and no other special circumstances existed to indicate that he could not have a fair trial without a lawyer.

It was now up to Gideon's Court-appointed lawyer to prove that his rights had really been violated without due process of law.

Abe Fortas, Gideon's Champion

The man selected by the Court to represent Gideon was one of Washington's most prestigious lawyers. His name was Abe Fortas. A member of the high-powered law firm of Arnold, Fortas, and Porter, Abe Fortas was a long-time friend and personal adviser to President Lyndon B. Johnson. He had been undersecretary of the Department of the Interior during President Franklin D. Roosevelt's New Deal administration. A lifelong liberal, Fortas was a champion of the underdog, although he was perhaps best known as a corporate lawyer and had made a fortune representing various businesses in dealings with the federal government. Some of Fortas's colleagues resented his flamboyance—he drove a Rolls Royce, for example—but none doubted his brilliance as a lawyer.

Fortas would not, of course, be paid for representing Gideon, but the case offered the kind of challenge that he could not resist.

Fortas's first move was to get a transcript of the trial at which Gideon had been sentenced to five years in Raiford Prison. Then he wrote to Gideon asking him to write in detail the story of his life.

As soon as he read the trial transcript Fortas became convinced that there had been half a dozen instances during the trial where even an adequate defense lawyer could have probably succeeded in convincing a judge and jury that Gideon should not be convicted. Gideon's autobiography, which came several weeks after Fortas had requested it, was an eye-opener. There seemed little question that Gideon was telling the unvarnished truth in giving the naked details of his life and his various clashes with the law. There also seemed little doubt that Gideon was an all but hopeless petty criminal repeater—or *recidivist*, as the professional penologists would put it. One could not help but ask, was Gideon worth all the trouble?

But Abe Fortas did not long debate such philosophical questions. He had appeared frequently enough before the Supreme Court and had practiced law in most other fields long enough to know that it was not the character of the litigant involved that should be debated but the validity of the point or points of law. And Fortas was firmly convinced that Gideon had been illegally deprived of his rights and that *Betts* v. *Brady* should be overthrown.

Although the Supreme Court had reversed earlier decisions about a hundred times before the Gideon case, Fortas knew it never did so lightly. But just a year earlier, in 1961, the Court had overturned a 1949 decision on illegal searches and seizures, so perhaps there was a mood for change in the air. (The illegal searches and seizures case, *Mapp* v. *Ohio,* is recounted in the next chapter.)

Fortas knew, however, that he could not depend upon moods. He could not depend upon anything, in fact, but a hard legal argument, to sway the justices. He began to prepare just such an argument.

Appearing for the State of Florida, opposing Gideon's request that his conviction be overturned, was Bruce R. Jacob, a young assistant attorney general. Jacob had never before appeared before the Supreme Court, but he welcomed the opportunity. Jacob planned to base his case largely on the long-established *Betts* v. *Brady* ruling.

The Gideon Supreme Court Hearing

Although Gideon's request for a rehearing arrived at the Supreme Court building on January 8, 1962, his case was not actually heard by the Court until more than a year later, January 15, 1963. The intervening twelve months had been filled with the selection of lawyers, the preparation of briefs or arguments by the lawyers, and the filing of their briefs with the Court so that the nine justices could read and study them. Then came the all-important oral hearings.

At the actual hearing Abe Fortas was the first to speak. Each lawyer had just one hour to present his case, plus ten minutes for rebuttal. Fortas wasted no time in getting to the heart of the matter. "This record does not indicate that Clarence Earl Gideon was a person of low intelligence," he said, "or that the judge was unfair to him. But to me this case shows the basic difficulty with *Betts* v. *Brady.* It shows that no man, however intelligent, can conduct his own defense adequately."

He then went on to point out that under the *Betts* v. *Brady* ruling there had to be "a case-by-case supervision by this Court of state criminal proceedings" to decide whether or not a poor person on trial was entitled to a free lawyer. Obviously, if the Court now decided that accused persons in all criminal cases, not just capital crime cases, must be provided with counsel, then the Supreme Court would no longer have brought before it cases such as Gideon's.

But the justices were obviously concerned that such a ruling might result in an overwhelming demand by all poor clients for lawyers in all cases.

Fortas pointed out that a lawyer would not have to be appointed for "petty offenses." It was his opinion, however, that a defendant should have a lawyer from the first time he was brought before a judge through his or her trial and any appeal.

"What about traffic violations?" one of the justices asked him.

Fortas said he thought lawyers could even be provided for traffic offenses, but he doubted that many such offenders would ask for a free lawyer. If they did, they could be turned over to the public defender.

"What you are saying," another justice said, "is that the right to counsel is assured by the Fourteenth Amendment."

Abe Fortas agreed.

Attorney Bruce Jacobs's emphasis was on states' rights as opposed to federal intervention in criminal cases. "By imposing an inflexible rule [that all defendants in all criminal cases were entitled to a lawyer]," Jacob said, "we feel this Court would be intruding into an area historically reserved to the states."

He also pointed out that any new ruling in place of *Betts* v. *Brady* would place tremendous burdens on the taxpayers. "Some poor defendants would demand other free defense services, perhaps even psychiatrists, expert consultants," and who knew what more. "In effect," he said, "this Court would be requiring the states to adopt socialism, or a [criminal] welfare program."

Jacob pointed out that the state of Florida now had more than five thousand convicts in its prisons who had been tried without counsel. All of these prisoners could be eligible for release if *Betts* v. *Brady* were overthrown. "If the Court does reverse," Jacob said, "we implore it to find some way not to make it retroactive. We have followed *Betts* in good faith."

The ruling in the case that was finally known as *Gideon* v. *Wainwright* (Louie L. Wainwright was the director of the Florida Division of Corrections at the time the case was heard by the Supreme Court) was announced on Monday March 18, 1963. The nine justices were unanimous in overruling *Betts* v. *Brady*. They did not rule on other problems that this decision created—whether or not the ruling was retroactive, for example. As a result, the individual states are still having problems with their prison population and how its members should be affected by the *Gideon* v. *Wainwright* ruling. Each state has handled the problem differently. Anthony Lewis described the situation in Florida in his book about the Gideon case, *Gideon's Trumpet,* as follows:

> Florida went ahead and applied the Gideon rule retrospectively, to all who had been convicted of felonies without counsel. The results were spectacular. By January 1, 1964, 976 prisoners had been released outright from Florida penitentiaries, the authorities feeling that they could not be successfully retried. Another 500 were back in the courts, and petitions from hundreds more were awaiting consideration.

Gideon himself was given a new trial, this time with a lawyer, W. Fred Turner, of Panama City. Once again the trial

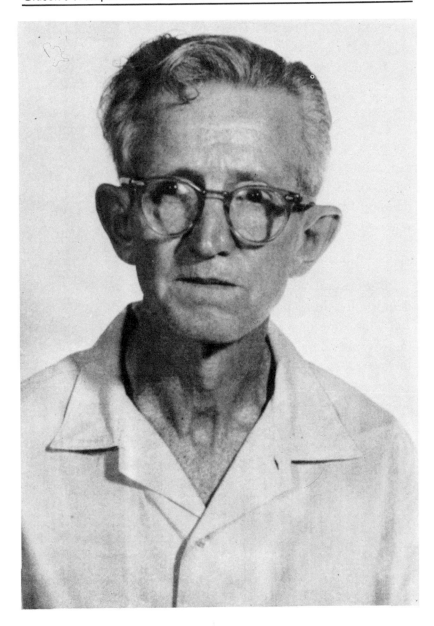

Clarence Earl Gideon at the time the Supreme Court ruled that penniless defendants are entitled to free counsel when charged with a major crime.

was held before Judge McCrary and a jury of six men. Gideon was found not guilty.

It would be good to be able to say that Clarence Earl Gideon went on to live an exemplary life for the rest of his days. He did write a letter filled with gratitude to Abe Fortas, but then Fortas did not hear from him again. Gideon continued his ways as a drifter, managing, however, to keep out of jail. For a time he lived in Fort Lauderdale, Florida, working at odd jobs in trailer parks and service stations. Once he was arrested for public drunkenness but paid a $30 fine and was released. Finally he drifted back to Hannibal, Missouri, where eventually he was hospitalized for tuberculosis and cancer. He died in 1972.

For several years there was not even a marker on Gideon's grave in Hannibal's Mount Olivet Cemetery. Then, in 1984, the American Civil Liberties Union remedied this situation by providing funds for a marker. "For $387 we marked the grave of a cantankerous man who taught us that the individual does make a big difference," commented Joyce Armstrong, executive director of the Eastern Missouri ACLU.

Perhaps the Mayor of Hannibal, John Lyng, best summed up Gideon's life and the Gideon case. After the gravesite ceremony when the marker was dedicated, Mayor Lyng, a former prosecutor, said, "Clarence Earl Gideon didn't live an exemplary life. He was a police problem when he lived here in Hannibal. But he exhibited one quality we all respect and admire—that is, being willing to do whatever is necessary to make a point when you think you're right."

Postscript: The Danny Escobedo Case

A slightly different version of the Gideon-type ruling was handed down by the Supreme Court in 1964. This resulted from the case of *Escobedo* v. *Illinois*.

Danny Escobedo was a Chicagoan who was convicted of murdering his brother-in-law in 1961. Escobedo was not a pauper. He could well afford a lawyer, but he claimed that his lawyer had been barred from a Chicago police station while Escobedo was in custody. Not having been allowed to see his lawyer, Escobedo had made a confession that was used at his trial.

In 1964 the Supreme Court reversed Escobedo's conviction and ordered his release from prison on the grounds that all criminal suspects have the right to an attorney while they are in police custody. The murder charges against Escobedo were then dropped.

Following his release from prison, Escobedo claimed he was being harassed by the police and tried to change his name. In 1968 he was again convicted of a felony—this time he was allowed to consult a lawyer—and was sentenced to 22 years in prison. His crime: selling narcotics.

Escobedo was paroled for good behavior in March of 1975. Parole officers later said he had made an "excellent adjustment to society" and had become a model parolee. Consequently, he was released from parole in 1978.

But in the fall of 1984 Danny Escobedo was back in the news. This time he was accused of molesting his twelve-year-old stepdaughter. Escobedo stoutly proclaimed his innocence. "I never molested the girl, believe me," he said. "I'm 46 years old. I don't believe in anything like that. I'm an old-fashioned man."

Despite his claim of innocence, Escobedo was found guilty by a jury. In October of 1984 he was sentenced by Judge Thomas Fitzgerald to twelve years in prison. Escobedo once again claimed that he had been denied his rights after being taken into custody on the molestation charge. This time he said he had been held for 26 hours without being read his

Miranda rights or without being allowed to make a phone call. Law enforcement officers denied this, and once again Escobedo was led away to jail—like Gideon a somewhat tarnished symbol of a landmark Supreme Court decision.

But shortly after his sentencing in this unsavory case Escobedo was released on bond while he appealed his conviction. In the fall of 1985 while he was out on bond Escobedo was once again arrested, this time for allegedly shooting a young man named Jesus Reyes outside a Chicago bar and allegedly firing at but missing another young man, Alfredo Reyes. When he surrendered to police, Escobedo made no comment.

And so the Escobedo saga continued.

8

Mapp v. Ohio

Before dawn on a May morning in 1957 a bomb blew the front porch off the home of Don King, a boxing promoter and alleged professional gambler, in Cleveland, Ohio. Several days later, a suspect in the bombing, Virgil Ogiltree, was reported to police to be hiding out in a two-family house on Cleveland's Milverton Road.

A Miss Dollree Mapp owned the Milverton Road house. According to the *Cleveland Press*, Miss Mapp was the former wife of one-time light heavyweight boxing champion Jimmy Bivans and was rumored in gossip columns to be the fiancée of light heavyweight champion Archie Moore.

The police went to the Mapp home and waited outside for a while for Ogiltree to emerge. When he did not, they went up to the house and knocked on the door. They were greeted by Dollree Mapp, who told them they could not enter without a search warrant.

Exactly what happened in the next several hours has since been the subject of much dispute. The police on duty at the Mapp home claimed they remained on duty there and radioed their headquarters for a search warrant to be delivered to them. Before long they again knocked on the Mapp door and announced that they had a search warrant. Dollree Mapp always claimed that what they had was a blank piece of paper.

What the police probably had was not the search warrant itself but an affidavit, which must be made out by police as the first step in securing a search warrant. In any event, what the paper actually was did not eventually make much difference, because when the time came for the "search warrant" to be produced in court it had somehow disappeared.

When the police knocked on the Mapp door the second time, this time with some sort of paper in hand, Miss Mapp again refused to let them in. The police then broke in, made their way upstairs to Dollree Mapp's apartment, and began to make a thorough search. When Mapp tried to stop them, the police handcuffed her.

During the course of the search of the Mapp apartment the police found what they described as "obscene materials"—pictures of nude men and women and several allegedly pornographic books. In the basement of the house they also found various kinds of gambling material, including betting forms. Along the way, hiding in the first floor apartment, the police also found the original subject of their search, Virgil Ogiltree, the suspected bomber.

When the police returned to headquarters they had Ogiltree with them. They also had taken into custody Dollree Mapp, whom they arrested for being in possession of illegal betting materials and the allegedly obscene pictures and books. The state of Ohio had recently passed a law making the possession of obscene materials illegal.

Dollree Mapp was almost immediately acquitted of the illegal betting materials charge (a misdemeanor), but she did not have her day in court regarding the obscenity charge (a

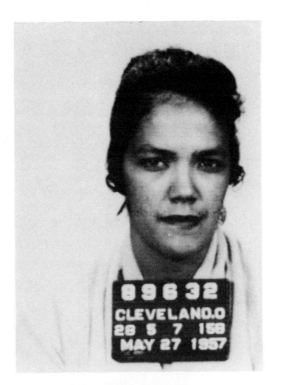

Cleveland police photos of Dollree Mapp. In a decision on the suit of *Mapp* v. *Ohio*, the Supreme Court upheld the Fourth Amendment right of an individual against illegal search and seizure.

felony) until more than a year later. In September of 1958 Miss Mapp was found guilty on the latter charge and sentenced to a term of from one to seven years in the Ohio State Reformatory for Women. At this trial it was reported that the "search warrant" was missing.

Interestingly, as several legal experts have since pointed out, any search warrant that might have been issued would have given the police the authority to search only for the alleged bomber, Virgil Ogiltree, and not for the obscene materials that they seized in their search. The basic legal question was whether the police had engaged in illegal search and seizure. If the police had seized the alleged obscene materials illegally—that is, without a warrant to look for them—could they be used in a trial against Dollree Mapp? She intended to find out by appealing her case. Meanwhile, she remained free on bail.

Appeal Based on Fourth Amendment

The law regarding illegal searches and seizures has a long and noble history in the United States. It goes back to colonial days. Before the American Revolution the colonists were forced to submit to having their homes invaded by officers of the British government searching for smuggled or untaxed goods and potential revolutionaries. They did so on the authority of permanent blanket warrants issued by the British king. This widespread use of blanket search warrants was one of the irritants that caused the colonists to rise up in revolt against the British crown.

When the Americans had won the Revolutionary War and began to form their own independent government, they made certain there would be no more illegal searches and seizures. They dealt with the matter by adding the Fourth Amendment to the U.S. Constitution.

The right of the people to be secure in their houses, papers and effects, against unreasonable searches and seizures, shall not be violated and no warrants shall issue, but upon probable cause, supported by oath or affirmation, and particularly describing the place to be searched, and the person or things to be seized at the time.

The Fourth Amendment has been a jealously guarded right of the American people ever since the eighteenth century, but from time to time it has had to be tested in the courts. The *Mapp* v. *Ohio* case was one of those times.

For some years immediately preceding Dollree Mapp's arrest, however, the state of Ohio had been weakening the Fourth Amendment by rarely using search warrants. In fact, in 1936 the Ohio Supreme Court had gone so far as to rule that the Fourth Amendment did not apply to the individual states. Although Ohio state law officially required search warrants, after 1936 they were seldom used. Consequently, any evidence obtained during an illegal search, such as that seized in Mapp's house, was automatically allowed to be used in a criminal trial if it was directly related to the case.

Mapp Case Reaches the Supreme Court

Dollree Mapp's conviction on the obscenity charge was first reviewed by the local country court of appeals. It upheld the conviction. The case was then appealed to the Ohio Supreme Court, which also refused to overturn the original verdict. Still determined that she was right, Mapp wanted to have her case heard by the U.S. Supreme Court.

All of these appeals took time and money. Nevertheless, Dollree Mapp borrowed the approximately $8,000 it would cost to carry her case to the nation's highest tribunal. The Supreme Court agreed to hear arguments in *Mapp* v. *Ohio* on March 29, 1961.

Mapp's lawyer was Alexander L. Kearns, a colorful champion of lost causes. Kearns succeeded in enlisting the aid of the American Civil Liberties Union. It was the ACLU's lawyer, Bernard Berkman, who made the most telling arguments in the *Mapp* v. *Ohio* case.

Berkman attacked not only the illegal search and seizure aspects of the Mapp conviction but also the Ohio obscenity statute itself. Claiming that the obscenity statute was unconstitutional under the First Amendment (freedom of speech), Berkman said, "Legislating action in the realm of morals must not infringe upon paramount individual rights. . . . We submit that interposing a policeman between a normal adult and his library is not a proper means of accomplishing what otherwise might be a valid legislative purpose."

Regarding illegal searches and seizures, Berkman simply reviewed the Fourth Amendment and how it had been applied in virtually all of the other states except Ohio in socalled criminal cases.

The state of Ohio was represented by Gertrude Bauer Mahon, an assistant county prosecutor, who upheld the legality of both the obscenity statute and the obtaining of obscene materials in the Mapp home. She said, "We feel that the Fourth Amendment's constitutional provision does not cancel out evidence of a criminal offense."

Several of the justices closely queried attorneys for both sides and then retired to consider their verdicts in *Mapp* v. *Ohio* as well as numerous other cases. Three months later, in July of 1961, they issued their ruling: Any evidence obtained through illegal search and seizure, or without a proper warrant, cannot be used as evidence in state courts. Dollree Mapp would not have to go to jail—at least not yet.

In reading the Court's decision, Justice Tom Clark said that the Constitution's Fourth Amendment definitely did apply to all of the states. Consequently, the Court could not stand by and permit the Fourth Amendment "to be revocable at the whim of any police officer who, in the name of law enforcement itself, chooses to suspend its enjoyment. Our decision, founded on reason and truth, gives to the individual no more than that which the Constitution guarantees him, to the police officer no less than that to which honest law enforcement is entitled, and, to the courts, that judicial integrity so necessary in the true administration of justice."

Dollree Mapp Does Go to Jail

Dollree Mapp, like Danny Escobedo and numerous others whose convictions have been overturned by the nation's highest tribunal, claimed that after the Supreme Court ruled in her favor police waged a vendetta against her. Whether or not this is true, she did eventually wind up in jail, this time on a drug charge.

After the Supreme Court decision Miss Mapp moved to New York City. There she sold and rented real estate and became the successful owner of a Harlem furniture store. Then, in 1973, the police came to her home in Queens looking for a drug suspect. They asked if they could search her place, and this time, unlike the earlier, similar situation in Cleveland, she readily allowed them to do so.

Miss Mapp later said she allowed the search because she felt she had nothing to hide. But in the apartment the police found an unregistered revolver. Miss Mapp said she had bought the gun for self-protection in Ohio and did not know she had to reregister it in New York. But the police also claimed to have found a rent receipt belonging to the drug suspect. Arrested and brought to trial on this and other circumstantial evidence, Miss Mapp was convicted on drug charges and sentenced to serve from twenty years to life at New York's Bedford Hills women's prison.

While in prison Miss Mapp organized a group called the Committee Against Life-for-Drugs, which eventually succeeded in getting the state legislature to revise the harsh sentencing of drug offenders. While working with this committee, Miss Mapp's case came to the attention of several prominent people who tried to get her sentence reduced. One of those who wrote a letter in her behalf was former U.S. Attorney General Ramsey Clark, son of Justice Tom Clark, who had read the Supreme Court's ruling in *Mapp* v. *Ohio*.

Finally, in 1981, after she had spent more than nine years in prison, Dollree Mapp's sentence was commuted by Governor Hugh Carey. After leaving prison she worked with prison inmates on a volunteer legal program and endeavored through state officials to obtain a full pardon for herself.

Mapp Ruling Modified

Since the *Mapp* v. *Ohio* ruling by the Supreme Court there has been a great deal of effort by law enforcement agencies to get the ruling somewhat modified. In 1984 the U.S. Senate passed a bill to limit the exclusion of evidence in criminal trials under certain circumstances. The substance of the bill was contained in the following sentence: "Evidence which is obtained as a result of a search and seizure and which is otherwise admissible shall not be excluded in a proceeding in a court of the United States if the search and seizure was undertaken in a reasonable, good faith belief that it was in conformity with the Fourth Amendment to the Constitution of the United States."

Since then the U.S. Supreme Court has also in several cases indicated that this "evidence obtained in good faith" modification should prevail as the law of the land. Obviously, many legal cases lie ahead in which this "good faith" idea will be debated, but there is no indication that the Court will fully reverse itself and return to the dark days before *Mapp* v. *Ohio.*

As Justice Felix Frankfurter once said, "A knock at the door, whether by day or night as a prelude to a search, without authority of law but solely on the authority of the police," should be "condemned as inconsistent with the conception of human rights enshrined in the history of the basic constitutional documents of English-speaking peoples." Any other attitude toward illegal searches and seizures is the attitude of the police states of totalitarian powers.

9

Religion in the Public Schools

One day in 1957 Ellory Schempp, the oldest son of Mr. and Mrs. Edward Schempp, came home from high school in the Philadelphia suburb of Abington and complained to his parents about having to take part in a daily religious exercise broadcast over the school's public address system. The Schempps were members of the Unitarian Universalist Church, whose creed "looks not to a perfect heaven but toward a good earth." Having to listen to Bible verses and recite the Lord's prayer in school was not in keeping with the Schempps' religious beliefs.

The administrators of Ellory's school, however, were simply acting in accordance with a Pennsylvania state law that required such religious exercises. Because the practice met with complaint from the Schempps as well as others, a federal court soon ruled that the required exercises were unconstitutional. The school then made the practice voluntary and everybody seemed satisfied—everybody, that is, except the Schempps.

During the daily religious exercise in high school Ellory Schempp refused to stand up. In addition, since students could voluntarily select the religious verses they wanted to read aloud, Ellory requested that he be allowed to read from the Koran, the holy book of the Moslems. Such rebellious actions eventually led to Ellory's being permanently excused from taking part in the daily religious exercise.

While this controversy simmered, Mr. and Mrs. Schempp made an effort to interest the American Civil Liberties Union in their case. But by the time the ACLU got around to taking any action Ellory had graduated. He then went on to attend Tufts College where he later was graduated cum laude and Phi Beta Kappa with a major in physics.

Meanwhile, the Schempps' two younger children, Donna and Roger, were still in the Abington high school, and they kept the controversy alive.

When the ACLU did become active in the Schempp case, its lawyers carried it all the way to the U.S. Supreme Court. Along the way several lower courts ruled in the Schempps' favor, and the Supreme Court eventually upheld the lower court rulings. In 1963 in the case of *School District of Abington Township* v. *Schempp* the Court outlawed Bible reading and the recitation of the Lord's Prayer in the nation's public schools—or thought it did.

Actually, the Schempp case was not the first case regarding compulsory or voluntary religious practices in the nation's classrooms. Nor is it likely to be the last, since the controversy continues to rage today.

How It All Began—The First Amendment

As it was with the matter of illegal searches and seizures, so it was with the early American colonists in the matter of the separation of church and state. Many colonists came to this country to escape religious persecution, so when the Founding

Fathers wrote the Constitution and agreed upon a Bill of Rights they made certain that the very first Amendment said:

> Congress shall make no law respecting an establishment of religion, or prohibiting the free exercise thereof. . . .

The decisive argument in the Schempp case, as it has been in all the other similar cases before and since, was that by permitting the Bible to be read and the Lord's Prayer to be recited in the public schools the government was to some degree effecting the establishment of a particular religion—in this case the Christian religion.

Interestingly, until relatively recent times the Supreme Court had to respond to few challenges regarding religious freedom in the United States. But in the twentieth century conflicts between church and state have steadily grown in number, and usually they have involved the public schools. Perhaps the most famous of these was what the newspapers of the day called the Scopes "Monkey Trial," in 1925. While the decision in this trial never actually reached the Supreme Court it is still frequently referred to in oral arguments before that Court today.

The Scopes "Monkey Trial"

John T. Scopes was a young teacher in Dayton, Tennessee. In his classroom Scopes taught Darwin's theory of natural selection, or the gradual evolution of plants, animals, and man. Not only did the parents of many of Scopes' students object to the teaching of evolution but there was also a Tennessee state law that prohibited "the teaching in any public school any theory that denies the story of the divine creation of man as taught in the Bible, and to teach instead that man has descended from a lower order of animals."

Scopes wasn't, of course, teaching that men and women were the direct descendants of monkeys, but his critics claimed he was and brought suit against him.

William Jennings Bryan was the attorney for the prosecution. Bryan was the greatest orator of his day. He had run unsuccessfully for president several times and had been secretary of state under President Woodrow Wilson. Like Scopes' critics, Bryan was a religious fundamentalist who not only claimed to know the Bible by heart but also claimed that every word in it was true.

Scopes' defense attorney was Clarence Darrow. Darrow was the most famous criminal lawyer of his day and a self-proclaimed agnostic, if not an outright atheist. Because he had defended so many poor and unfortunate clients, Darrow was frequently referred to as "the attorney for the damned." Scopes was not exactly damned, but there were many Tennesseans who thought Scopes and their children would be if he did not stop teaching them evolution.

All through the long, hot summer of 1925 the Scopes trial was conducted in what amounted to a carnival atmosphere in the stifling Dayton courtroom. That was before the days of air conditioning, and reporters from all over the United States jammed the proceedings in heat that was well over 100 degrees Fahrenheit. One of the nation's first radio broadcasts of a news event was also made from just outside the courtroom.

The trial was not many days old before the news media had transformed the "Monkey Trial" from a trial of Scopes and his teachings into a trial of prosecuting attorney Bryan and his rigid fundamentalist religious beliefs. Darrow was also responsible for the shift in emphasis, because, as he later wrote, he was convinced that if he could make a fool of Bryan and his beliefs the jury would have to acquit Scopes.

When Darrow finally succeeded in getting Bryan on the witness stand he asked him if he believed that every word in the Bible was literally true. Bryan said he did. Darrow then proceeded to point out certain parts of the Bible that simply would not stand up to either common sense or scientific scrutiny. Among these were Eve's being created from Adam's rib, Jonah's being swallowed by a whale and living to tell about it, the creation of the world in exactly seven days, and numerous others.

When Bryan continued to stand his ground, Darrow said bluntly, "You refuse to choose between your crude, impossible beliefs and the common intelligence of modern times."

In general, public sympathy seemed to be on Scopes' and Darrow's side, but it was the people of Tennessee who had the last laugh. The jury found Scopes guilty. The judge, however, only fined Scopes $100. But Scopes, of course, did not continue to teach in Dayton.

Darrow threatened to carry the case to the U.S. Supreme Court. He would do so, he said, "Because I think this case will be remembered as the first case of its kind since we stopped trying people in New England for witchcraft."

In the end it was not necessary to appeal the case beyond the Tennessee Supreme Court, which reversed the Scopes trial decision. A short time later the state of Arkansas made an attempt to enforce its own antievolution law, and this case did reach the U.S. Supreme Court. The nation's highest tribunal promptly ruled that all such laws were unconstitutional based on the First Amendment.

But the antievolutionists have not given up in their effort to keep the teaching of evolution out of the public schools. For example, textbook companies have been pressured to give equal space in science books to the theory of evolution and the Biblical story of creation. In at least two important instances, however, this effort has backfired on both the fundamentalists and the textbook publishers. In 1982 New York City removed high school biology texts by several publishers from the city's approved list because they de-emphasized or completely eliminated any mention of the theory of evolution. And as recently as late 1985 the California state board of education rejected every seventh and eighth grade science textbook offered by the nation's major textbook publishers, saying they had watered down sections on evolution simply to pacify believers in the Biblical story of creation.

During its 1986–87 session the Supreme Court was scheduled to rule on the legality of teaching creationism in the nation's public schools. The ruling would be based on deciding whether or not a Louisiana state law passed in 1981 was constitutional. The Louisiana law is called the "Balanced Treatment for Creation-Science and Evolution-Science Act."

In opposition to the continued teaching of creationism, the National Academy of Sciences, some 17 state academies of science, and 72 American winners of Nobel prizes filed briefs urging the Supreme Court to find that the Louisiana law and others like it violate the First Amendment to the Constitution by requiring the teaching of a religious doctrine in the public schools.

The Flag Salute Cases

The struggle over keeping religion out of the public school classrooms has also been waged in several other areas. One of these was in the so-called Flag Salute cases, which were notable for the Supreme Court's reversing one of its decisions in the short space of just three years, the most rapid reversal it has ever made.

To most casual observers, the decision of whether or not public school students should be required to salute the American flag and recite the Pledge of Allegiance to that flag would hardly be thought to involve the question of introducing religion into the classroom. But Mr. and Mrs. Walter Gobitis and their children thought otherwise.

Mr. and Mrs. Gobitis and their two young children, Lillian and William, lived in Minersville, Pennsylvania. They were members of an extremely strict religious faith, the Jehovah's Witnesses.

One day in 1936 Lillian and William Gobitis, somewhat as Ellory Schempp would do some years later, came home from school and complained to their parents that in their elementary school they were being forced to break the rules of their religion. But this had nothing to do with reciting Bible verses and repeating the Lord's prayer, to which they probably would not have objected. It had to do with saluting the flag and reciting the Pledge of Allegiance. In doing so, the Gobitis children felt, they were breaking several of the Ten Commandments. The Commandments in question were:

> Thou shalt have no other gods before me.
> Thou shalt not make unto thee any graven image, or
>   any likeness of any thing that is in the heavens
>   above, or that is in the earth beneath, or that
>   is in the water under the earth.
> Thou shalt not bow down thyself to them, nor serve
>   them.

The Gobitis children did not want to be unpatriotic, but they honestly felt the American flag was a graven image that they were being required to worship before God. And what was more, their parents agreed with them. They approved of Lillian and William's decision to refuse to take part in the flag salute ceremony.

A short time later the school superintendent, Charles E. Roudabush, called on Mr. and Mrs. Gobitis and told them that the Minersville Board of Education had agreed that the salute to the flag was a school rule and that if Lillian and William continued to break that rule they would be expelled.

"So be it," said Mr. and Mrs. Gobitis.

Supported by the members of his church, Mr. Gobitis then brought suit against the Minersville Board of Education. In his suit Gobitis pointed out that school attendance was compulsory in Pennsylvania and the Minersville school authorities were preventing him and his wife from following the law. He also stated that he had no objection to the flag salute ceremony itself, but he did object to his children's being forced to take part in it.

The Walter Gobitis claim was upheld by the Federal District Court in Philadelphia. The case was then appealed to the U.S. Circuit Court of Appeals, which also supported Gobitis. Determined to prove its point, the Minersville Board of Education had its lawyer carry the case to the U.S. Supreme Court.

By now the Gobitis case had gained national attention. The time was 1939, and World War II had just broken out in Europe. Lawyers from the American Civil Liberties Union and the American Bar Association volunteered to represent the Gobitis family before the Supreme Court. In doing so, they pointed out to the justices that the Minersville school authorities had violated the Gobitis children's civil liberties just as Adolf Hitler and Benito Mussolini were violating civil liberties in Europe.

But despite such pleas for the upholding of American democratic principles, on June 3, 1940, the Supreme Court ruled against the Gobitis family. In its ruling the Court said simply that the Minersville School Board had the authority to require a specific school program and "the flag salute is an allowable portion of a school program."

The decision in the Gobitis case did not end the flag salute dispute, however. Within a matter of months a similar situation arose in nearby West Virginia.

Jehovah's Witnesses Fall Out of Favor

While there had been a considerable amount of public sympathy for the members of the Gobitis family when the Supreme Court ruled against them, the sympathy quickly evaporated after the United States entered World War II in December 1941. Following the Japanese attack on Pearl Harbor, patriotic fervor reached fever pitch, and anyone who would even consider refusing to salute the American flag was generally regarded as a traitor.

In the midst of this fervor, in 1942, the West Virginia State Board of Education declared that all of the state's public schools must "make the salute of the American flag a regular part of the school program activities." Further, any students refusing to salute the flag would be expelled and their parents would be liable to prosecution.

Immediately many Jehovah's Witnesses risked prosecution by instructing their children to refuse to take part in any flag salute ceremony. At that point the protesting Jehovah's Witnesses had fallen into disfavor with many Americans. Most young members of the faith who were of draft age had refused to serve in the nation's military forces, claiming exemption on the grounds that they were conscientious objectors. As a result, several Jehovah's Witnesses' meetings were broken up and their meeting places set afire. Several states even went so far as to pass laws outlawing the faith, which was clearly an unconstitutional measure.

Fuel was added to the fires of intolerance when a Jehovah's Witness named Walter Barnette and several other members of the faith sought an injunction against the West Virginia flag salute order in the Charleston Federal District Court. They sought the injunction on the grounds that the order was unconstitutional because it was "a denial of religious freedom and free speech."

Their case, *West Virginia State Board of Education* v. *Barnette,* reached the Supreme Court in March 1943. By that time the justices had clearly had a change of heart and mind. Several of them had never been satisfied with the Court's ruling in the Gobitis case, and they had had ample opportunity to consider their own failings in that instance.

Finally, on June 14, 1943, which by a curious coincidence was national Flag Day, they handed down their ruling. It was a complete reversal of the earlier ruling in the Gobitis case. Justice Robert H. Jackson read the majority opinion, stating:

> To sustain the compulsory flag salute we are required to say that a Bill of Rights which guards the individual's right to speak his own mind left it open to public authorities to compel him to utter what is not in his mind.
>
> Those who begin coercive elimination of dissent soon find themselves exterminating dissenters. Compulsory unification of opinion achieves only the unanimity of the graveyard. It seems trite but necessary to say that the First Amendment was designed to avoid these ends by avoiding these beginnings.
>
> If there is any fixed star in our constitutional constellation, it is that no official, high or petty, can prescribe what shall be orthodox in politics, nationalism, religion, or other matters of opinion or force citizens to confess by word or act their faith therein. If there are any circumstances which permit an exception, they do not now occur to us.

Prayer in the Classroom

The question of the constitutionality of prayer and Bible reading in the public school classroom did not become a full-fledged debate until well after World War II. Then, in 1948, the Supreme Court ruled that a course in religious education in the public schools at Champaign, Illinois, was unconstitutional. Despite that ruling, surveys taken by the National Education Association in the 1950s indicated that at least a third of the states allowed classroom prayers. A similar survey made in the early 1960s showed that a third of the nation's school districts not merely allowed classroom prayers but required them. Most of these schools also approved of classroom Bible reading.

It was in the midst of this situation that the Schempp case occurred. But even while the Schempp dispute was making its way through the courts another case arose in New York State that resulted in the Supreme Court's ruling that public school prayer was in violation of the First Amendment. This was the case of *Engel* v. *Vitale,* which was the first school prayer case to reach the Supreme Court.

Engel v. *Vitale*

Actually, the Engel case was somewhat tied in with the flag salute ceremony. In 1958 the New York State Board of Regents issued a short prayer that could be recited by public school students. The Herricks school system on Long Island not only adopted the prayer but also made a regular daily custom of having its students recite the prayer each morning right after they observed the salute to the flag.

The prayer was a simple one and apparently harmless. It read, "Almighty God we acknowledge our dependence on Thee, and we beg Thy blessings upon us, our parents, our teachers, and our country."

But simple and apparently harmless as the prayer was there were certain parents who objected to having their children recite it. One of those who objected was Lawrence Roth, who later said in a newspaper interview, "My basic feeling was that if the state could tell our children what to pray and when to pray and how to pray, there was no stopping."

Roth and several of his friends succeeded in interesting the American Civil Liberties Union in their case, and suit was brought against the State of New York and the local Herricks school board, whose president was William Vitale, Jr. Stephen Engel, a friend of Roth's, was one of several petitioners who brought the suit, and alphabetically his name came first on the suit.

The first hearing in the *Engel* v. *Vitale* case took place in the Nassau County Court House before Judge Bernard S. Meyer. It took Meyer six months to render a decision, and when he did so he came down in favor of the Herricks school board. Although Meyer's written opinion filled almost seventy pages, what it boiled down to was that he could not see how the short prayer violated any child's constitutional rights since it was not actually compulsory. (School Board President Vitale had always emphasized that any child not wanting to recite the prayer definitely did not have to do so.)

Engel, Roth, and the other petitioners then appealed the case to the appellate court and the New York State Court of Appeals, both of which upheld Judge Meyer. Engel and Roth were determined to carry the case to the Supreme Court, but because the Schempp case and several others were also being considered for hearings it was not certain that *Engel* v. *Vitale* would even be considered. Finally, however, the high tribunal agreed to hear the case during its 1961–1962 term.

The ACLU lawyer, William Butler, based his oral presentation to the Supreme Court justices on the argument that actually the so-called Regents' Prayer *was* compulsory. In support of this argument he said, "Would the little child . . . leave the classroom; or would the parent be expected to ask the school system to excuse his child, who may be singled out as a nonconformist? I must adopt Mr. Justice Frankfurter's thesis . . . that the law of imitation applies. Little children want to be with other little children. . . . The effect would be to cast upon this child's mind some indelible mark, and I think it can be sustained that, in effect, the children are coerced into saying this prayer, because of these reasons."

Counsel for the Herricks school board, Bertram Daiker, reemphasized the fact that participating in the prayer was not compulsory and that no request for a student to be excused from such participation had ever been made. He then went on:

"Since the earliest days of this country, going back to the Mayflower Compact, the men who put the country together have publicly and repeatedly recognized the existence of a Supreme Being, a God. When, therefore, we say this prayer, which . . . is an avowal of faith . . . which recognizes that there is some Supreme power, some Supreme Being, we are proceeding fully in accord with the tradition and heritage that has been handed down to us." Daiker also pointed out that a prayer was used before the opening of each session of the Supreme Court, adding, "We are not trying here in the Herricks School District to teach religion any more than the prayer used in this Court."

School Prayer Ban Causes Furor

The ruling in *Engel* v. *Vitale* was handed down in June of 1962. When it came it was a shocker, at least so far as the

Earl Warren was Chief Justice in 1962 when the Supreme Court ruled that prayer in the public schools violated the First Amendment.

media were concerned. The majority of the justices had agreed that the Herricks school prayer, no matter how short, violated the First Amendment. Newspapers across the country ran headlines that read: SCHOOL PRAYER UNCONSTITUTIONAL, BAN PRAYER IN PUBLIC SCHOOLS, and SCHOOL PRAYER HELD ILLEGAL.

Few Supreme Court decisions have caused so much public outcry as those in the *Engel* v. *Vitale* and the *Abington Township* v. *Schempp* cases, the latter following hard on the heels of the Engel decision. Legislators said the Court had "struck a death blow against all believers in a Supreme Being," and warned against the "destruction of the religious and spiritual life of this country." One church even displayed on its outdoor bulletin board the inflammatory statement, CONGRATULATIONS COMMUNIST RUSSIA!

Saner voices, including that of the president of the United States, tried to prevail. President John F. Kennedy, a devout Catholic, said: "It is important for us if we are going to maintain our constitutional principle, that we support the Supreme Court decisions, even when we may not agree with them. In addition, we have in this case a very easy remedy, and that is to pray ourselves."

Gradually the furor over the banning of prayer in the public school classrooms of the nation died down, but it definitely did not die out. In fact there has continued to be a steady groundswell of opinion in favor of getting the Supreme Court to reverse its opinion on the subject.

Much of this effort has been on the part of fundamentalist religious leaders as well as their followers. A secular organization, the Moral Majority, headed by fundamentalist preacher Jerry Falwell, also tried to move the debate into the political arena. In this Falwell was backed by some legislators, including Republican Senator Jesse Helms of North Carolina.

In the summer of 1985 Senator Helms tried to take the matter of school prayer out of the hands of the judiciary and turn it over to the nation's legislators. Helms introduced into the Senate a bill that would deny not only the Supreme Court but also all Federal courts the authority to rule on cases involving prayer, Bible reading, and religious meetings in public schools. The bill was defeated by a large majority of the Senators, but Helms said he was not giving up the fight. He left little doubt that the nation would be hearing from him and his followers again, this time at the polling booth. Helms noted that the Senators who had voted against his bill would be targeted for defeat in the elections of 1986 by fundamentalists who supported the Helms proposal. Actually, the fall elections did little to prove or disprove Helms' prediction.

Helms, Falwell, the Moral Majority, and other pro-prayer organization members had powerful support from the president of the United States. Chief Executive Ronald Reagan had long made known his desire "to get prayer back in the schools" and stated at one point that even a moment of silence at the beginning of each school day to allow each student to repeat a silent prayer or otherwise engage in self-contemplation would be a step in the right direction. Opponents of this idea, including Senator Lowell Weicker of Connecticut, said such a "step" would simply be a foot-in-the-door toward legitimizing spoken classroom prayer and Bible reading. Weicker also pointed out, as did others, that there was nothing to stop students or anybody else from praying silently whenever they wanted to.

Whether the Constitutional matter of the separation of church and state should be decided in this political fashion was debatable, but even the Founding Fathers would have had to agree that it was a perfect example of the American democratic political process at work. Nevertheless, the Supreme Court remains the court of last resort in guarding that process. For even if Helms and his followers were to succeed in passing pro-prayer legislation and get it signed by the president, the Supreme Court could always declare such legislation unconstitutional.

10

The Supreme Court's First Antinuclear Decision

Karen Silkwood was a lively, fun-loving young woman of twenty-six when she took a job on August 5, 1972, with the Kerr-McGee Corporation's nuclear facility in Cimarron, just outside Oklahoma City. Although the job, helping to make plutonium fuel pellets for a nuclear reactor, only paid $3.45 an hour, Karen was delighted to get it. The recently divorced mother of three children who were living with their father, she had been considering supporting herself with a job as a secretary when the opportunity to be a laboratory technician with Kerr-McGee came along. Having taken high school and college courses in advanced chemistry, physics, and radiology, Karen had always wanted some sort of career in the science field. This, she thought, was her golden opportunity.

Unfortunately, it did not take Karen very long to become disillusioned with her job. For one thing she did not think safety precautions at the plant were adequate. In addition, as she told one of her sisters on a brief visit to her home in Nederland, Texas, none of her supervisors were actually scientists. "A lot of them don't know as much as I do about the job," she said.

Karen Silkwood had been born and brought up in Nederland in southeast Texas. She had also attended nearby Lamar University while living at home, but she had not graduated. Instead, while she was still a teenager she had fallen in love with an older boy, Bill Meadows, and they had eloped. Actually, they had not been married, but they told Karen's parents they had had a ceremony performed by a justice of the peace.

Karen and Bill had lived together for seven years as common-law man and wife, and Karen had given birth to three children, a son and two daughters. Bill was a machinist and made good money but was something of a vagabond and a spendthrift. During the seven years they lived in half a dozen Texas and Oklahoma towns and Karen had to find jobs as clerk, receptionist, and secretary to help pay the bills that her husband constantly ran up. In addition to the fact that she had excellent grades in high school and college, Karen was an extremely attractive young woman, so she never seemed to have any trouble getting jobs.

Finally, when Bill started an affair with Karen's best girlfriend, Karen left him. Despite the fact that the couple had not been legally married, a divorce was necessary according to Texas law. Karen very much wanted to keep the children, but she thought they should have both a mother and father and decided that Bill and her former girlfriend could best fill those roles. But Karen insisted that she be allowed to visit her children whenever she wanted to and that they be allowed to visit her frequently.

Following the divorce, Karen resumed her maiden name of Silkwood and went to stay with another girlfriend in Oklahoma City. The friend worked at the local medical center and told Karen she could get her a job as a secretary there. But once she was in Oklahoma City Karen became intrigued with the possibility of getting a job with the huge Kerr-McGee

Karen Silkwood in 1974, about the time she was exposed to radioactive material at the Kerr-McGee plant where she was employed. Karen was secretly compiling a list of safety infractions to give to top union officials.

Corporation. She applied for a job as a clerk or secretary, but when her high school and college transcripts indicated she had had advanced science courses she was offered a job as a lab technician at Kerr-McGee's nearby Cimarron nuclear plant.

The Cimarron plant was named after the Cimarron River, which was within walking distance to the north. The site had been selected by the Kerr-McGee Corporation when it had been given a multimillion-dollar contract by the U.S. Atomic Energy Commission (AEC) to manufacture fuel rods for nuclear reactors. When Karen went to work there, the Cimarron facility was making plutonium fuel rods for a new kind of nuclear reactor, called a "fast-breeder," at Hanford, Washington.

Labor Unrest Leads to Strike

In addition to what Karen saw as the lack of safety precautions and what she regarded as lack of training on the part of the supervisory personnel, there was also a considerable amount of labor unrest at the Cimarron plant. At the end of November in 1972, only a few months after Karen had been hired, the local chapter of the plant union, the Oil, Chemical, and Atomic Workers (OCAW), called a strike. The OCAW contract had just expired, and the union was demanding more money and better safety measures for its workers. When Kerr-McGee refused to offer new terms, OCAW called a strike and Karen went out with a number of her coworkers. She came from a long line of loyal OCAW family members who had worked in the Texas oil fields, and her loyalties were solidly on the side of the union.

But Kerr-McGee was a tough company to buck. It had not even allowed OCAW into its several plants until 1966 and since then had successfully refused to give in to union demands despite several strikes. This time was no exception.

After several months the strikers were told that if they did not return to work their jobs would be given to others. When the strike collapsed, Karen reluctantly returned to work.

Karen soon found that very little had changed inside the plant. Safety measures were as lax as ever, she believed. But soon she was given a small promotion, and she tried to ignore what she saw as glaring flaws in the safety precautions as well as in the training of the supervisors. One day a woman co-worker fainted in the lab, and Karen was angered to see that the health aid who was supposed to take charge in such emergencies did not even know how to break open a vial of smelling salts. In addition, when an oxygen tank arrived, it did not function. Finally the stricken woman was taken away by ambulance attendants.

Following this incident and several others in which she believed that she and other workers were actually exposed to radioactivity, Karen decided to become more active in the company union. During the strike she had gotten acquainted with Jack Tice, one of the local union leaders. Now she told Tice she was willing to play a role in calling the infractions of safety regulations to the attention of Atomic Energy Commission officials. Tice agreed that she should compile a list of such infractions, and when it was completed he would arrange for her to meet with top union officers in Washington, D.C., and then, if the evidence merited it, with officials of the AEC.

It took Karen several months to compile her list. By the early fall of 1974 when she and Tice went to Washington, Karen had noted some thirty-nine safety and health infractions that included everything from uranium dust in the employees' lunchroom to spills of radioactive material in the labs to contaminated glove boxes. Glove boxes were supposedly exposure-proof containers into which workers thrust their glove-encased hands to polish plutonium pellets.

The OCAW officers were impressed with Karen's list, but they insisted that before any direct action could be taken with the AEC they needed hard proof. Karen said she could get such proof. It involved what she said was the cover-up of the faulty welding of the plutonium fuel rods that were being manufactured for nuclear reactors—the Cimarron plant's principle function. Karen said that lab technicians had been told to disguise defects by grinding down any signs of such things as hairline fractures.

If she could get evidence of these claims, the OCAW officers told her, the AEC would be forced to act. How could she get it?

Karen explained that there were highly magnified pictures called photomicrographs taken of the faulty rods before and after they were ground down and "fixed."

Could she get copies of these photomicrographs?

Karen said she would get the originals.

How?

By stealing them.

Karen Silkwood—Spy

It was agreed that within two months Karen would gather photomicrographs showing the allegedly doctored fuel rods plus any other incriminating evidence she could find. At the end of that time she could turn the material over to Steve Wodka, a top union representative who would come to Oklahoma to pick it up.

For the next six weeks Karen secretly gathered material from the Cimarron plant's files. Then, in November of 1974, shortly before she was to meet with Wodka, Karen became mysteriously involved in several contamination incidents. One occurred after she had been working in a glove box. She apparently was washed free of the contamination, but later a laboratory monitor indicated she was still radioactive. When the source of her contamination could not be found, AEC inspectors were brought in. Eventually, they returned with Karen to her apartment, where they found high levels of contamination, especially in the kitchen refrigerator. Their findings raised the suspicion that some way, accidentally or otherwise, Karen had been bringing plutonium home with her. Why such a thing had occurred no one seemed sure.

Finally, Kerr-McGee officers agreed that Karen should be flown to the scientific laboratory at Los Alamos, New Mexico, to be tested for radioactive internal-body contaminants. This delayed her meeting with union leader Steve Wodka. But at the end of a week the Los Alamos technicians reported Karen was virtually free of any contaminants, and she returned to Oklahoma and her job at the Cimarron plant. She also made plans to meet with Wodka and turn over her manila envelope of "incriminating findings" to him.

Upon her return, Karen's apartment was still under quarantine, so she stayed with her boyfriend, Drew Stephens. Until now she had not told Drew of her spy activity. Now she did and added that Wodka was bringing with him a reporter, David Burnham, from *The New York Times,* who could call the case to public attention. Drew tried to talk her out of going through with the meeting, but Karen flatly refused to listen to him. Instead she asked him to do her a favor. She had a union meeting early that evening, and Wodka and Burnham were arriving by plane at 6:30. Would Drew pick them up and take them to a motel? Drew agreed to do so.

Karen Silkwood's Mysterious Death

Drew Stephens met Steve Wodka and David Burnham at the Oklahoma City airport and then took them to a nearby Holiday Inn motel, where Karen was to join them after her union meeting. Karen left the union meeting about seven-thirty, got into her white Honda Civic in the parking lot, and headed out onto the highway toward Oklahoma City. That was the last anybody was to see of her alive. But several of her coworkers who saw her leave the meeting said she had been carrying a large manila envelope with her.

About an hour later a truck driver rolling along the same highway spotted a small white car lying on its side just off the road, near a concrete culvert. The truck driver braked his rig to a stop, climbed down from his cab, and hurried back to the accident scene. Although the car was partially hidden by the culvert, the truck driver was able to see its lone occupant, a woman, smashed against the steering wheel. Karen Silkwood was dead. Later, the truck driver also reported that among the car's contents scattered near the accident scene he had seen a manila envelope, its contents partially spilled on the ground.

It was another hour before the men at the motel who had been awaiting Karen's arrival were informed of the fatal accident. They too hurried to the scene, but by this time the state police were in charge and had cordoned off the area. The police, however, said they had found no manila envelope or any other important papers.

Almost immediately questions began to arise about Karen Silkwood's mysterious death. The fact that it had happened while she was on the way to deliver what she apparently thought was incriminating evidence against the Kerr-McGee health and safety practices at the Cimarron plant caused many to wonder at the curious coincidence of the accident. The missing envelope added to the speculation.

Several amateur investigators later claimed that Karen's car had been forced off the road by another car right at the spot where it would smash into the culvert. But no proof was ever found for this bizarre theory. The official police report stated that Karen's death was an accident, that she had become drowsy while driving—perhaps from taking sedatives—and her car had simply careened off the road. Not only the amateur investigators but also Karen's friends scoffed at this theory. Those who last saw her said she was all keyed up with excitement when she left the union meeting. What happened to the manila envelope, if there was an envelope, has never been determined. In fact, many aspects of Karen Silkwood's mysterious death remain unresolved to this day.

Karen's Family Sues Kerr-McGee

Karen's family, especially her father, Bill Silkwood, were never satisfied with the findings in Karen's death. The only recourse they had, however, was to bring suit against the Kerr-McGee Corporation for Karen's having suffered from radiation contamination at the Cimarron plant in November of 1974.

The jury trial in Oklahoma City lasted for three months. At the trial Karen's father and her three children were represented by attorneys who called upon several witnesses from the Cimarron plant. Their testimony strongly implied that the plant did not always comply with safety regulations as set down by the Nuclear Regulatory Commission (NRC).

It was also alleged that Kerr-McGee was negligent regarding worker safety. No one had actually caught the company in safety infractions, but the Silkwood attorneys claimed that plant supervisors had endangered both the workers and the local community. If this was true, the judge told the jurors, punitive damages could be awarded. "The basis for allowance of punitive damages," the judge said, "rests upon the principle that they are allowed as a punishment to the offender for the general benefit of society, both as a restraint upon the transgressor and as a warning and example to deter the commission of like offenses in the future."

But the Kerr-McGee lawyers argued that according to the Atomic Energy Act of 1954 only the Federal government, the NRC in the Silkwood case, had any right to punish those who broke nuclear safety laws. Thus, they claimed, punitive damages would be illegal.

But the jury was not influenced by the Kerr-McGee attorneys' arguments. It found Kerr-McGee guilty as charged, awarding the Silkwood estate $500,000 for the late Karen's personal contamination injuries, and $10 million in punitive damages for "recklessness" in exposing Karen and others to danger.

Kerr-McGee immediately appealed the two awards to the U.S. Court of Appeals. That court ruled against the Silkwoods, dismissing the $500,000 personal injury award on the grounds that it was work-related and therefore could be paid only under the Oklahoma state workers' compensation law. The $10 million punitive award was dismissed on the grounds that a jury and the state could not regulate nuclear safety; this was a Federal responsibility.

The Silkwood attorneys thereupon appealed to the Court of Appeals' ruling to the U.S. Supreme Court.

The Supreme Court's Silkwood Case Ruling

The Supreme Court did not hand down its ruling in the Silkwood case until January of 1984. When it did so it ruled in favor of the Silkwoods, but not unanimously. The majority decision was divided among the justices five to four.

Justice Byron White read the ruling. He read that the Court rejected the argument that Federal law prohibited state-authorized awards of punitive damages because the Federal government has exclusive control over the licensing and

Bill Silkwood, Karen's father, outside the Supreme Court Building. After Karen's mysterious death, Karen's family sued Kerr-McGee over Karen's personal contamination injuries. The Supreme Court ruled in 1984 in favor of the Silkwoods, and in 1986 Kerr-McGee and Karen's heirs finally settled the suit.

regulation of nuclear power. "It is difficult to believe," Justice White said, "that Congress would, without comment, remove all means of judicial recourse for those injured by illegal conduct."

It was truly a landmark ruling, because for the first time the Court had rendered what amounted to an antinuclear decision. Up to that time the Court had steadily upheld the idea that the regulation of nuclear safety was strictly the responsibility of the federal government. This meant that states and private citizens on a jury did not have the right to assess punitive damages against offenders and thus establish regulatory policy at the local level. The Silkwood decision had changed all that.

The decision would have powerful effects not only on the state regulation of existing nuclear energy plants but also on the location and building of new ones. It would also play a role in letting the states decide whether or not they wanted nuclear waste deposited within their borders and if so where the waste repository sites should be. Needless to say, the Silkwood decision could have important ramifications throughout the nuclear industry for years to come.

But the ruling in the Silkwood case was a divided decision, and there was always the possibility that in similar future cases the Supreme Court could reverse itself. This was what the Reagan administration was working for, since its legal officials still held that the federal government has exclusive control over both the licensing and regulation of nuclear power. They would be fought every step of the way, however, by most of the states. This was indicated by the fact that in the Silkwood case no fewer than sixteen states entered briefs on the side of the Silkwoods. Such briefs are called *amicus curiae,* or friends of the court. There is little doubt that the Supreme Court had been influenced by this powerful representation on the part of the states.

Silkwood Suit Settled

Meanwhile, it appeared that it might be some years, if ever, before the Silkwood family actually collected any money. In effect the Supreme Court's decision returned the case to the Appeals Court for another round of hearings. Kerr-McGee contested the appeals case on the grounds that the award of punitive damages was excessive and based on insufficient evidence. It then seemed possible that this could result in a new trial. James Ikard, the family lawyer, predicted the case might not be resolved for another three years. But in the summer of 1986 Karen Silkwood's heirs and Kerr-McGee finally settled the suit. The energy company agreed to pay Karen's estate $1.38 million, with the company admitting no guilt for the automobile accident that killed Karen.

11

The Future of the Supreme Court

Much of the future of the Supreme Court depends, of course, on the kinds of cases that are brought before it. The Court itself does not initiate any legal cases. It purely and simply reacts to those cases which are brought before it in which decisions have already been rendered by lower courts. Then, based on the nine justices' interpretation of the U.S. Constitution, a ruling is rendered.

But as 1987, the Bicentennial year for the Constitution, approached, there were numerous signs that the makeup of the high tribunal was about to be radically changed. Several of the justices were reaching an advanced age when illness and death would inevitably remove them from the bench. In 1985 the average age of the Burger Supreme Court was seventy. The majority of the justices were more than seventy-six years old, and by 1986 the nation would have the oldest Supreme Court in history. Up to that time the oldest was the Court that served during President Franklin D. Roosevelt's administration.

The Reagan administration left little doubt that it was dissatisfied with the liberal nature of the existing Court and would fill all available vacancies with conservative appointees. The trend was clear in the appointments of lower level Federal court judges. Since taking office in 1981, President Reagan had appointed 42 of the 168 appeals court judges and 160 of the 575 district court judges. All of these appointees had conservative credentials.

Reagan's success in remolding the Federal judicial system along his own conservative lines did not go without criticism. Liberal critics have claimed that potential judicial nominees have been subjected to intensive and undue scrutiny on such issues as abortion, school prayer, affirmative action, and the use of busing for school desegregation. Senator Paul Simon of Illinois, a member of the Judiciary Committee, expressed concern that political ideology appeared to have become the sole basis for the administration's rejection of nominees.

Such criticism, of course, has been launched against every president since George Washington, who was not only the first president but also the first president to try to get a Supreme Court filled with justices who were sympathetic to his political philosophy. And it should not be forgotten that the Senate still has its say in whatever judicial appointments the president makes. For judicial appointments at lower Federal court levels the Senate rarely rejects presidential nominees unless the nominee is incompetent or tainted by scandal. But at the Supreme Court level the Senate has rejected one in five nominees, including one of George Washington's. So it still has a powerful voice in the matter.

A New Chief Justice

On June 17, 1986, Chief Justice Warren Burger, seventy-eight, announced his retirement from the Court. As head of the Federal Commission on the Bicentennial of the U.S. Constitution, he wanted to devote all his energies to plans for the 1987 celebration.

President Reagan nominated Associate Justice William Rehnquist, sixty-one, to be the new Chief Justice and nominated Judge Antonin Scalia, fifty, to become an associate justice. Their appointments were confirmed by the Senate in the fall of 1986, and they were sworn in on September 26, 1986.

None of the older members of the Court, all over seventy-five, gave any indication of a willingness to retire, although Justice Lewis Powell might eventually be forced from the bench because of illness. Justices Harry Blackmun and Thurgood Marshall continued to be physically active. Although far from well, Marshall said, "I was appointed for life and intend to serve my term." William Brennan, the oldest of the justices, was also among the spryest and mentally alert. The younger associate justices—Byron White, Sandra Day O'Connor, John Paul Stevens, and Antonin Scalia—were all in good health.

Longevity and sticking at their jobs has long been a tradition among Supreme Court justices, so today's Court members are in good company. Over 30 of the 105 justices have worked past their seventy-fifth birthdays. Among them have been such memorable figures as John Marshall, Roger Taney, Oliver Wendell Holmes, and Louis Brandeis. John Harlan was almost blind at the end of his tenure at age seventy-two, but constitutional scholars have nevertheless called him "one of the greatest justices in history" during his final years.

Disability and death—as they come to all men and women—must come to today's justices. But thanks to the Founding Fathers who wrought so well in creating the U.S. Constitution, the nation will weather their loss as they are replaced by men and women of equal stature no matter what their political leanings.

The Supreme Court justices pictured here are Sandra Day O'Connor, Lewis Powell, Thurgood Marshall, William Brennan, Jr., Chief Justice William Rehnquist, Byron White, Harry Blackmun, John Paul Stevens, and Antonin Scalia.

U.S. Supreme Court Justices

Name	Term	Appointed by
CHIEF JUSTICES		
John Jay	1790-1795	Washington
John Rutledge	1795	†Washington
Oliver Ellsworth	1796-1800	Washington
John Marshall	1801-1835	J. Adams
Roger B. Taney	1836-1864	Jackson
Salmon P. Chase	1864-1873	Lincoln
Morrison R. Waite	1874-1888	Grant
Melville W. Fuller	1888-1910	Cleveland
Edward D. White	1910-1921	Taft
William H. Taft	1921-1930	Harding
Charles E. Hughes	1930-1941	Hoover
Harlan F. Stone	1941-1946	F. D. Roosevelt
Frederick M. Vinson	1946-1953	Truman
Earl Warren	1953-1969	Eisenhower
Warren E. Burger	1969-1986	Nixon
William H. Rehnquist	1986-	Reagan
ASSOCIATE JUSTICES		
James Wilson	1789-1798	Washington
John Rutledge	1790-1791	Washington
William Cushing	1790-1810	Washington
John Blair	1790-1796	Washington
James Iredell	1790-1799	Washington
Thomas Johnson	1792-1793	Washington
William Paterson	1793-1806	Washington
Samuel Chase	1796-1811	Washington
Bushrod Washington	1799-1829	J. Adams
Alfred Moore	1800-1804	J. Adams
William Johnson	1804-1834	Jefferson
H. Brockholst Livingston	1807-1823	Jefferson
Thomas Todd	1807-1826	Jefferson
Gabriel Duvall	1811-1835	Madison
Joseph Story	1812-1845	Madison
Smith Thompson	1823-1843	Monroe
Robert Trimble	1826-1828	J.Q. Adams
John McLean	1830-1861	Jackson
Henry Baldwin	1830-1844	Jackson
James M. Wayne	1835-1867	Jackson
Philip P. Barbour	1836-1841	Jackson
John Catron	1837-1865	Van Buren
John McKinley	1838-1852	Van Buren
Peter V. Daniel	1842-1860	Van Buren
Samuel Nelson	1845-1872	Tyler
Levi Woodbury	1845-1851	Polk
Robert C. Grier	1846-1870	Polk
Benjamin R. Curtis	1851-1857	Fillmore
John A. Campbell	1853-1861	Pierce
Nathan Clifford	1858-1881	Buchanan
Noah H. Swayne	1862-1881	Lincoln
Samuel F. Miller	1862-1890	Lincoln
David Davis	1862-1877	Lincoln

† appointment not
confirmed by Senate

Stephen J. Field	1863-1897	Lincoln
William Strong	1870-1880	Grant
Joseph P. Bradley	1870-1892	Grant
Ward Hunt	1873-1882	Grant
John M. Harlan	1877-1911	Hayes
William B. Woods	1881-1887	Hayes
Stanley Matthews	1881-1889	Garfield
Horace Gray	1882-1902	Arthur
Samuel Blatchford	1882-1893	Arthur
Lucius Q. C. Lamar	1888-1893	Cleveland
David J. Brewer	1890-1910	Harrison
Henry B. Brown	1891-1906	Harrison
George Shiras, Jr.	1892-1903	Harrison
Howell E. Jackson	1893-1895	Harrison
Edward D. White	1894-1910	Cleveland
Rufus W. Peckham	1896-1909	Cleveland
Joseph McKenna	1898-1925	McKinley
Oliver W. Holmes, Jr.	1902-1932	T. Roosevelt
William R. Day	1903-1922	T. Roosevelt
William H. Moody	1906-1910	T. Roosevelt
Horace H. Lurton	1910-1914	Taft
Charles E. Hughes	1910-1916	Taft
Willis Van Devanter	1911-1937	Taft
Joseph R. Lamar	1911-1916	Taft
Mahlon Pitney	1912-1922	Taft
James C. McReynolds	1914-1941	Wilson
Louis D. Brandeis	1916-1939	Wilson
John H. Clarke	1916-1922	Wilson
George Sutherland	1922-1938	Harding
Pierce Butler	1923-1939	Harding
Edward T. Sanford	1923-1930	Harding
Harlan F. Stone	1925-1941	Coolidge
Owen J. Roberts	1930-1945	Hoover
Benjamin N. Cardozo	1932-1938	Hoover
Hugo L. Black	1937-1971	F.D. Roosevelt
Stanley F. Reed	1938-1957	F.D. Roosevelt
Felix Frankfurter	1939-1962	F.D. Roosevelt
William O. Douglas	1939-1975	F.D. Roosevelt
Frank Murphy	1940-1949	F.D. Roosevelt
James F. Byrnes	1941-1942	F.D. Roosevelt
Robert H. Jackson	1941-1954	F.D. Roosevelt
Wiley B. Rutledge	1943-1949	F.D. Roosevelt
Harold H. Burton	1945-1958	Truman
Tom C. Clark	1949-1967	Truman
Sherman Minton	1949-1956	Truman
John M. Harlan	1955-1971	Eisenhower
William J. Brennan, Jr.	1956-	Eisenhower
Charles E. Whittaker	1957-1962	Eisenhower
Potter Stewart	1958-1981	Eisenhower
Byron R. White	1962-	Kennedy
Arthur J. Goldberg	1962-1965	Kennedy
Abe Fortas	1965-1969	Johnson
Thurgood Marshall	1967-	Johnson
Harry A. Blackmun	1970-	Nixon
Lewis F. Powell, Jr.	1972-	Nixon
William H. Rehnquist	1972-	Nixon
John P. Stevens	1975-	Ford
Sandra Day O'Connor	1981-	Reagan
Antonin Scalia	1986-	Reagan

Further Reading

Berger, Raoul. *Congress v. The Supreme Court*, Boston: Harvard University Press, 1969. (Paperback), New York: Bantam Books, 1973.

Bowen, Catherine Drinker. *Miracle in Philadelphia: The Story of the Constitutional Convention, May to September 1787*, Boston: Atlantic Monthly Press, 1986.

Cullop, Floyd G. *The Constitution of the United States: An Introduction*, New York: New American Library, 1984.

Farrand, Max. *The Framing of the Constitution of the United States*, New Haven: Yale University Press, 1913.

Fisher, Louis. *Politics of Shared Powers*, Washington: Congressional Quarterly Press, 1981.

Friendly, Fred W. and Elliott, Martha J.H. *The Constitution, That Delicate Balance*, New York: Random House, 1984 (Paper).

Garraty, John A. (editor). *Quarrels That Have Shaped the Constitution*, New York: Harper Torchbooks, Harper & Row, 1975 (Paper).

Hamilton, Alexander, James Madison, and John Jay. *The Federalist Papers*, ed. with an introduction by Clinton Rossitor, New York: New American Library, 1961. (especially Numbers 47-51).

Hyman, Harold M. and Wiecek, William M. *Equal Justice Under Law, Constitutional Development 1835-1875*, New York: Harper & Row, 1982.

Kelly, Alfred H. and Harbison, Winifred A. *The American Constitution, Its Origins and Development*, New York: W.W. Norton, 1963.

Kohn, Howard. *Who Killed Karen Silkwood?*, New York: Summit Books (Simon & Schuster), 1981 (Paper).

Lawson, Don. *The Changing Face of the Constitution*, New York, London: Franklin Watts, 1979.

Lewis, Anthony. *Gideon's Trumpet*, New York: Vintage Books (Alfred A. Knopf and Random House), 1964 (Paper).

Lindop, Edmund. *Birth of the Constitution*, Hillside, N.J.: Enslow, 1987.

McKlosky, Robert Green. *The Modern Supreme Court*, Cambridge: Harvard University Press, 1972.

Morison, Samuel Eliot. *The Oxford History of the American People*, New York: Oxford University Press, 1965.

Pyle, Christopher H. and Richard M. Pious. *The President, Congress, and the Constitution*, New York: The Free Press, 1984.

Salomon, Leon I. *The Supreme Court*, Vol. 33, *The Reference Shelf*, New York: H.W. Wilson, 1961

Schwartz, Bernard. *A Basic History of the Supreme Court*, Princeton: Van Nostrand, 1968.

Stevens, Leonard. *Equal: The Case of Integration vs. Jim Crow*, New York: Coward, McCann & Geoghegan, 1975.

——. *Salute: The Case of the Bible Versus the Flag*, New York: Coward, McCann & Geoghegan, 1973.

——. *Trespass: The People's Privacy vs. Power of the Police*, New York: Coward, McCann & Geoghegan, 1977.

Tribe, Laurence H. *God Save This Honorable Court: How the Choice of Justices Can Change Our Lives*, New York: Random House, 1985.

Weiss, Ann. *The Supreme Court*, Hillside, N.J.: Enslow, 1987.

Index